THE DEMOCRATIC
WORKER-OWNED FIRM

THE DEMOCRATIC WORKER-OWNED FIRM

A NEW MODEL FOR THE EAST AND WEST

DAVID P. ELLERMAN

Industrial Cooperative Association,
Employee Ownership Services, and
Tufts University

Boston

UNWIN HYMAN

London Sydney Wellington

© David P. Ellerman 1990
This book is copyright under the Berne Convention. No
reproduction without permission. All rights reserved. This
book was typeset, proofed, and passed for press by the author.

Unwin Hyman, Inc.,
8 Winchester Place, Winchester, Mass. 01890, USA

Published by the Academic Division of
Unwin Hyman Ltd
15/17 Broadwick Street, London W1V 1FP, UK

Allen & Unwin (Australia) Ltd,
8 Napier Street, North Sydney, NSW 2060, Australia

Allen & Unwin (New Zealand) Ltd in association with the
Port Nicholson Press Ltd,
Compusales Building, 75 Ghuznee Street, Wellington 1,
New Zealand.

First published in 1990

Library of Congress Cataloging-in-Publication Data
Ellerman, David P.
    The democratic worker-owned firm: a new model for the
    East and West / David P. Ellerman.
        p.   cm.
    Includes bibliographical references.
    ISBN 0-04-445743-X
    1. Employee ownership. 2. Management--Employee
participation. 3. Comparative economics. I. Title.
HD5650.E4 1990   89-49337
338.6--dc20   CIP

British Library Cataloguing in Publication Data
Ellerman, David P.
    The democratic worker-owned firm: a new model for the
    East and West
    1. Industries. Collective ownership by personnel   I. Title
    082 388.6
    ISBN 0-04-445743-X

Typeset in 10 on 12 point Palatino by the author
Printed in Great Britain by Billing & Sons Ltd, Worcester

To

The Industrial Cooperative Association

—the fruitful union of theory and practice.

CONTENTS

Contents

Contents

Introduction

Capitalism, Socialism, and Economic Democracy

A *democratic firm* (also "democratic worker-owned firm" or "labor-based democratic firm") is a company "owned" and controlled by all the people working in it—just as a democratic government at the city, state, or national level is controlled by all of its citizens. In each case, those who manage or govern are ultimately responsible not to some absentee or outside parties but to the people being managed or governed. Those who are governed vote, on a one-person/one-vote basis, to directly or indirectly elect those who govern.

A market economy where the predominant number of firms are democratic firms is called an *economic democracy* (see Dahl, 1985; Lutz and Lux, 1988).

This book is about the ideas, structures, and principles involved in the democratic firm and in economic democracy. The book develops new concepts or, rather, applies old concepts to new situations—such as the "very idea" of applying democratic principles to the workplace. The material is not technically demanding in terms of economic theory but it may occasionally be conceptually demanding.

Old words may be used in new ways. For instance, "capitalism" is often taken as referring to a private property market economy—but an "economic democracy," where most firms are democratic firms, is also a private property market economy. The distinguishing feature of a capitalist economy *vis-à-vis* an economic democracy is the *employer–employee relation*—the legal relation for the voluntary renting or hiring of human beings.

The commodity that is traded in the labor market is labor services, or hours of labor. The corresponding price is the wage per hour. We can think of the wage per hour as the price at which the firm rents the services of a worker, or the rental rate for labor. We do not have asset prices in the labor market because workers cannot be bought or sold

1

in modern societies; they can only be rented. (In a society with slavery, the asset price would be the price of a slave.) [Fischer, et. al. 1988, p. 323]

In a democratic firm, work in the firm qualifies one for membership in the firm. The employment relation is replaced by the membership relation.

In ordinary language, "capitalism" is not a precisely defined technical term; it is a molecular cluster concept which ties together such institutions and activities as private property, free markets, and entrepreneurship as well as the employer–employee relationship.

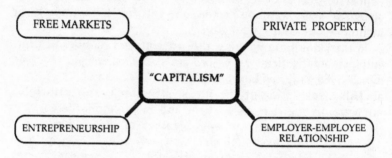

Figure A "Capitalism" as a Cluster Concept

There has also been a rather far-fetched attempt to correlate "capitalism" with "democracy." But this does not result from any serious intellectual argument that the employer–employee relation (which used to be called the "master–servant relation") embodies democracy in the workplace. The spurious correlation of capitalism and democracy seems to be the result of the bipolar debate between capitalism and socialism—where socialism, particularly in its Marxist–Leninist variety, is undemocratic both in the firm and in the political sphere.

Our normative critique is not of "capitalism" *per se* but of the employment relation or contract, so it must be sharply distinguished from a critique of private property (quite the opposite in fact), entrepreneurship, or free markets. In an economic democracy, there would be private property, free markets, and entrepreneurship—but "employment" would be replaced by democratic membership in the firm where one works.

The more subtle point is that the abolition of the employment relation does, nevertheless, make a change in property, markets, and entrepreneurship. This point can be illustrated by considering the related abolition of the master–*slave* relationship as an involuntary *or voluntary* relation. In a slavery system, "private property" included property in human beings and property in slave plantations. "Markets" included slave markets and it even included voluntary self-sale contracts. "Entrepreneurship" meant developing more and better slave plantations. Thus slavery could not be abolished while private property, free markets, and entrepreneurship remained unchanged. The abolition of slavery did not abolish these other institutions but it did change their scope and nature.

In the same fashion, we will see that the abolition of the employment relation in favor of people being universally the owners/members of the companies where they work would not abolish private property, free markets, or entrepreneurship—but it would change the scope and nature of these institutions.

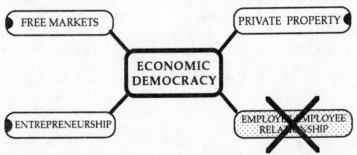

Figure B Employment Relation Abolition and Implied Changes

This leaves us with a linguistic problem. How do we refer to the economic system we are recommending to be changed in the direction of economic democracy? The word "capitalism" evokes private property, free markets, and entrepreneurship which are not being criticized here. Yet there is no other widely accepted word that focuses attention specifically on the employment relation. Expressions such as "wage slavery" or "wagery" are too rhetorical. "Wage system" is currently used to refer to fixed wages as opposed to so-called "profit-sharing." But "profit-sharing" is only a variable wage rate geared to a measure of performance, and it, like a piece-rate, is well within the confines of the employer–employee relationship.

We will therefore use bland expressions such as "employment system" or "employer–employee system"—when we are being careful—to refer to the system where work is legally organized on the basis of the employer–employee relation (with a private or public employer). Since the employment relation is so widespread (e.g. part of both capitalism and socialism), "employment" has also become synonymous with "having a job." We assume the reader understands that when we argue against the employment relation (in favor of universal membership in the firm) we are not arguing that everyone should be "unemployed"!

Linguistic habits die hard—for the author as well. When the word "capitalism" is nonetheless used in this book, it will be used *not* as a cluster concept to include private property, free markets, entrepreneurship, and Motherhood, but as a technical term to refer to an economy where almost all labor is conducted under the employment contract.

In America, "socialism" is means "state socialism"—an economy where almost all firms are owned and operated by some level of government. In socialist countries, in the Third World, and even in Europe, there are occasional attempts to redefine "socialism"—to move from the notion of "state socialism" towards "self-management socialism" which contemplates worker self-managed or democratic firms operating within a political framework of multi-party political democracy. Such a linguistic redefinition makes no sense in America. In the United States, "*state* socialism" is a redundant expression like "*red* tomato juice"—tomato juice only comes in one color and that color is red.

It is an open question outside of America whether there is any real point in trying to redefine and salvage the word "socialism." Economic democracy does not promote government ownership as desirable, only as a grudging necessity in some sectors (e.g. in the United States). Any notion of "socialism" that similarly did not promote government ownership would be

4

so different from what has been taken as "socialism" for over a century that there seems to be no rational reason in clinging to the word.   Nevertheless, non-rational reasons often predominate in politics. The economic reforms currently under way in the socialist world—such as *perestroika* in the Soviet Union—will certainly be *called* a new form of "socialism."

We will describe trends in these reforms towards economic democracy (which might in the socialist countries be called "self-management socialism" or "democratic socialism"). But there are also trends towards simply privatizing the government-employment system to a private-employment system, i.e. trends from state-socialism (or "public enterprise capitalism") towards conventional private enterprise capitalism. The socialist reforms are still pregnant with many possibilities—including a collapse back to authoritarian socialism.

Outline of the Approach

This book takes a comprehensive approach to the theory and practice of the democratic firm—from philosophical first principles to legal theory and finally down to some of the details of financial structure. The topics covered include:

— a descriptive analysis of the property rights involved in capitalist production, and a prescriptive application of the *labor theory of property* arguing for a democratic firm, since in such a firm people jointly appropriate the positive and negative fruits of their labor;
— a descriptive analysis of the governance rights involved in a capitalist firm, and a prescriptive application of *democratic theory* arguing for a democratic firm, since in such a firm people realize the right of democratic self-determination in the workplace;
— an extended discussion of the legal structure of the *democratic firm*—particularly of the system of *internal capital accounts* which corrects one of the central flaws in existing worker self-managed firms as in Yugoslavia;
— description and analysis of the system of *Mondragon worker cooperatives*;

— description and analysis of the American phenomena of employee stock ownership plans or *ESOPs*; and

— a description of a *hybrid democratic firm* that combines some of the best ideas from Mondragon-type worker cooperatives and from the American ESOPs in a simple form that can be transplanted to other countries.

We then turn to the enterprise reform programs currently under way across the socialist world. The topics include:

— a brief description and analysis of the "first *perestroika*," the forty–year–old *Yugoslavian experiment* in self-managed socialism and the accompanying problems generated by the ghost of state socialism in the form of "social property";

— a description of the *reforms in China* where the family farm (a democratic micro-firm) has emerged in agriculture and thousands of ad hoc worker stock experiments have sprung up in industry (reforms that are stalled and may be aborted during the post-Tiananmen-Massacre period);

— a description of the current revitalization of worker co-operatives, the emergence of over a thousand "lease firms" (workers leasing enterprises from the state), and the new worker buyouts from the state as part of *perestroika in the Soviet Union*;

— a brief analysis of the problems in Hungary's 1968 New Economic Mechanism and of the current efforts moving to-wards *worker ownership experiments* and *public capital markets*; and

— a brief description of the *self-management idea in Poland* that developed both in Solidarity and in new groupings of workers' councils between enterprises.

The overall perspective is that a new type of economic enterprise, the democratic firm, is at last coming into clear focus. It is different from both the traditional capitalist and socialist firms. Indeed, there are forces and principles at work in both systems that are pushing towards convergence on the common ground of economic democracy.

PART I

Theory of the Democratic Firm

1
The Labor Theory of Property

Property Rights and the Firm

This book presents a new analysis of capitalism. The analysis is new to the conventional stylized debate between capitalism and socialism. But the ideas are not new. The labor theory of property, democratic theory, and inalienable rights theory are part of the humanist and rationalist tradition of the Enlightenment.

The theory of the democratic worker-owned firm walks on two legs. That is, it rests on two principles.

(1) The property structure of the democratic firm is based on the principle that people have a natural and inalienable right to the fruits of their labor.
(2) The governance structure of the democratic firm is based on the principle that people have a natural and inalienable right to democratic self-determination.

This chapter deals with the *labor theory of property* (the fruits-of-their-labor principle) while the next chapter deals with the application of *democratic theory* to the firm.

The Fundamental Myth about Private Property

The understanding of what private property is and what it is not—is clouded in both capitalist and socialist societies by a

"Fundamental Myth" accepted by both sides in the capitalism/socialism debate. The myth can be crudely stated as the belief that "being the firm" is a structural part of the bundle of property rights referred to as "ownership of the means of production." A better statement and understanding of the myth requires some analysis.

Consider any legal party that operates as a capitalist firm, e.g. a conventional company in the United States or the United Kingdom that produces some product. That legal party actually plays two distinct roles:

— the *capital-owner role* of owning the means of production (the capital assets such as the equipment and plant) used in the production process; and
— the *residual claimant role* of bearing the costs of the inputs used-up in the production process (e.g. the material inputs, the labor costs, and the used-up services of the capital assets) and owning the produced outputs. The "residual" that is claimed in the "residual claimant" role is the economic profit, the value of the produced outputs minus the value of the used-up inputs.

The Fundamental Myth can now be stated in more precise terms. It is the myth that the residual claimant's role is part of the property rights owned in the capital-owner's role, i.e. part of the "ownership of the means of production." The great debate over the public or private ownership of the residual claimant's role is quite beside the point since there is no "ownership" of that role in the first place.

It is simple to show that the two roles of residual claimant and capital-owner can be separated without changing the ownership of the means of production. *Rent out the capital assets*. If the means of production such as the plant and equipment are leased out to another legal party, then the leasor retains the ownership of the means of production (the capital-owner role) but the leasee renting the assets would then have the residual claimant's role for the production process using those capital assets. The leasee would then bear the costs of the used-up capital services (which are paid for in the lease payments) and the other inputs costs, and that party would own the produced outputs. Thus the residual claimant's role is *not*

10

part of the ownership of the means of production. The Fundamental Myth is indeed a myth.

Who is to be the residual claimant? How is the identity of that party legally determined—if not by the ownership of the means of production? The answer is that it is determined by the direction of the contracts. The residual claimant is the hiring party, the legal party who ends up hiring (or already owning) all the necessary inputs for the productive operations. Thus that party bears the costs of the inputs consumed in the business operations, and thus that party has the legal claim on the produced outputs. The residual claimant is therefore a *contractual role*, not an ownership right that is part of the ownership of the means of production.

The ownership of the capital assets is quite relevant to the question of *bargaining power*; it gives the legal party with the capital-owner's role substantial bargaining power to also acquire the contractual role of residual claimancy. But there is no violation of the "sacred rights" of private property if other market participants change the balance of bargaining power so that the capital assets can only be remuneratively employed by being leased out. Markets are double-edged swords.

Understanding the Fundamental Myth forces a re-appraisal of certain stock phrases such as "ownership of the firm." That usually refers to the *combination* of the capital-owner's role and the residual claimant's role. But residual claimancy isn't something that is "owned"; it is a contractual role. What actually happens when party A sells the "ownership of the firm" to party B? Party A sells the capital assets owned in the capital-owner's role to B, and then B tries to take over A's contractual role as the hiring party by re-negotiating or re-assigning all the input contracts from A to B. Party A cannot "sell" the willingness on the part of the various input suppliers to re-negotiate or renew the contracts. Thus A's contractual role as the previous residual claimant cannot be "sold" as a piece of property like the capital assets. If B could not successfully take over the contractual role of residual claimancy, then it would be clear that by "buying the firm," B in fact only bought the capital assets. Thus buying the capital assets is not a sufficient condition to "become the firm" in the sense of becoming the residual claimant.

11

Buying the capital assets is also not a necessary condition for becoming the firm. A rearrangement of the input contracts could result in a new party becoming the residual claimant of the production process using the capital assets without there being any sale of the capital assets. The prime example is a *contract reversal* between the owners of the capital and the workers. We will later discuss examples where worker-owned firms are established by leasing the capital assets from the legal party that previously operated as the residual claimant in the production process using those assets. For example, this sometimes happens in distressed companies when the capital-owner no longer wants the residual claimant's role. It also happens in the Soviet Union and China when the means of production in certain enterprises are leased to the collectivity of workers.

Contract reversals can also go the other way. For example, the physical assets of many gas stations are owned by large oil companies that lease the assets to individuals as independent operators. During the Middle East oil embargo a number of years ago, gas prices shot up and long lines developed at gas stations. The gas stations became potential profit centers for the oil companies so some companies decided to reverse the contracts. Some oil companies terminated the leases and offered to hire the previously independent operators as employees to run the stations. One independent operator in Texas made the national news by barricading himself in the station and refusing to accept the new arrangement. He said to the oil company, "You can't do that; you have to buy me out." He thought he "owned the firm" in the sense of "owning" the residual claimant's role. The oil company would have to "buy the firm" from him. But, alas, one doesn't own a contractual role, and the oil company had more than enough bargaining power to reverse the contracts (with him or someone else as the station manager).

Thus "ownership of the means of production" is neither necessary nor sufficient to being the firm in the sense of being the residual claimant in the production process using those means of production. Contrary to the Fundamental Myth, being the firm is not part of the ownership of the means of production.

12

Ownership of a Corporation is not "Ownership of the Firm"

The logical structure of the above argument is, of course, independent of the legal packaging used by the capital owner, e.g. is independent of whether the capital is owned·by a natural person or by a corporation. Thus understanding the Fundamental Myth also allows us to understand what is and what is not a part of the bundle of property rights called "ownership of a corporation."

Suppose an individual owns a machine, a "widget-maker." It is easy to see how that ownership is independent of the residual claimant's role in production using the widget-maker. The capital owner could hire in workers to operate the widget-maker and to produce widgets—or the widget-maker could be hired out to some other party to produce widgets.

That is a simple argument to understand. But it is amazing how many economists and lawyers (not to mention lesser souls) suddenly cannot understand the argument when the individual is replaced by a corporation. Indeed, suppose the same individual incorporates a company and issues all the stock to himself in return for the widget-maker. Now instead of directly owning the widget-maker, he is the sole owner of a corporation that owns the widget-maker. Clearly this legal repackaging changes nothing in the argument about separating capital ownership and residual claimancy. The corporation has the capital-owner's role and—depending on the direction of the hiring contracts—may or may not have the residual claimant's role in the production process using the widget-maker. The corporation (instead of the individual) could hire in workers to use the widget-maker to manufacture widgets, or the corporation could lease out the widget-maker to some other party.

The legal ownership of the corporation only guarantees the capital-owner's role. The residual claimant's role could change hands through contract rearrangements or reversals without the ownership of the corporation changing hands. Therefore the ownership of the corporation is not the "ownership of the firm" where the latter means the residual claimant's role in the production process using the corporation's capital assets (e.g. the widget-maker). The idea that the repackaging of the

13

machine-owner's role as corporate ownership is a transubstantiation of capital ownership into "ownership" of the residual claimant's role is only another version of the Fundamental Myth.

The Appropriation of Property

Property rights are born, transferred, used, and will eventually die. In *production*, old property rights die and new property rights are born; in *exchange*, property rights are transferred. In production, the new property rights to the outputs are born or initiated. The acquisition of the initial or first-time property right to an asset is called the "appropriation" of the asset. Property rights die (i.e. are terminated) when the property is consumed or otherwise used up. In production, it is the property rights to the inputs (materials and services of capital and labor) that are terminated. When a property right is terminated that is a negative form of appropriation; it can be termed the appropriation *of the liability* for the used-up property.

In production, there is the appropriation of the assets produced as outputs and the appropriation of the liabilities for the used-up inputs. Some symbolism can be used to capture the idea. Consider a simple description of a production process where the people working in the enterprise perform the labor services L that use up the inputs K to produce the outputs Q. Thus the produced outputs are Q and liabilities for the inputs could be represented by the negative quantities $-K$ and $-L$. Let us represent these three quantities in a list where the quantities are given in the order:

(outputs, inputs, labor).

Then the list (or "vector") giving the assets and liabilities appropriated in the production process is given by what will be called the:

$$whole\ product = (Q, -K, -L)$$

14

("whole" because it includes the negative as well as the positive results of production).

There is a descriptive and a normative question about property appropriation:

— *Descriptive Question*: In a private property market economy, how is it that one legal party rather than another legally appropriates the whole product of a technically-described production process?

— *Normative Question*: Which legal party ought to legally appropriate the whole product of a technically-described production process?

We have already answered the descriptive question. "Legally appropriating the whole product" is a property-oriented description of the residual claimant's role:

> Whole Product Appropriator
> = Residual Claimant.

We saw that residual claimancy was contractually determined by being the hiring party. The hiring party hires or already owns all the inputs services used up in production (i.e. K and L) so that party, as it were, appropriates the liabilities -K and -L. Hence that party certainly has the legally defensible claim on the produced outputs (i.e. Q). In that manner, the contractually determined hiring party legally appropriates the whole product (Q, –K, –L) of the production process.

Perhaps the only surprise in the above argument is that the property rights to the whole product (i.e. the property rights behind residual claimancy) are *not* part of the ownership of the means of production, i.e. are not part of the capital-owner's role. The capital owner may or may not legally appropriate the whole product (i.e. be the residual claimant) depending on the direction of the hiring contracts.

For example, let K be the services of the widget-maker per time period, let L be the labor that uses up the services K to produce the widgets Q. If the corporation that owns the widget-maker hires in the labor services L, then it will have the claim on the widgets Q, so the corporation will appropriate the whole product (Q, –K, –L). If the corporation leases out the widget-maker (i.e. sells the services K) to some other party who hires or already owns the labor L, then that party will be able to claim Q and thus legally appropriate the same whole product (Q, –K, –L). The idea that the appropriation of the whole product is somehow an intrinsic part of the ownership of the widget-maker is only another version of the Fundamental Myth.

The Normative Question of Appropriation

What is the traditional *normative* basis for private property appropriation? The natural basis for private property appropriation is *labor*—people's natural and inalienable right to the (positive and negative) fruits of their labor (see Ellerman, 1985a for a discussion of John Locke's theory of property). That is the traditional labor theory of property (see Schlatter, 1951).

We will develop the argument that in any given productive enterprise, the liabilities for the used-up inputs are the negative fruits of the labor of the people working in the enterprise (always including managers). The produced outputs are the positive fruits of their labor. The democratic worker-owned firm is the type of enterprise where the people working in it are the legal members of the firm so they then legally appropriate the positive and negative fruits of their labor. Hence we will argue that the labor theory of property—the natural basis for private property appropriation—implies worker-owned firms, not traditional capitalist firms.

We previously saw that as a matter of descriptive fact, the appropriation of the whole product was not part of the private ownership of the means of production. We now will argue that as a matter of normative principle, the whole product should be appropriated by the people who produced it, the people working in the enterprise. Thus, it is private property itself—when refounded on its natural basis of labor—that implies democratic worker-ownership.

This labor theoretic argument finds a resonance in both capitalist and socialist thought. That dual resonance has always

16

been associated with John Locke's theory of property. Some interpreted it as the foundation of private property, while others took it as a forerunner to radical theories arguing for some form of "socialism" based on worker self-management. There is merit in both interpretations. We turn now to the labor theory of property as it has been interpreted and misinterpreted in socialist thought.

"The Labor Theory" of Value—or of Property

At least since Marx's time, any discussion of the labor theory of property in socialist thought has been dominated by Marx's labor theory of value and exploitation. The labor theory of property simply has not had an independent intellectual life. Yet many of the ideas underlying the support and interpretation of the "labor theory of value" actually are based on the labor theory of property. Hence it is best to speak firstly of "The Labor Theory" (LT) as a primordial theoretical soup without specifying "of Value" or "of Property." Then the various overtones and undercurrents in LT can be classified as leaning towards *the labor theory of value* (= LTV) or *the labor theory of property* (= LTP).

Since so much of the literature is formulated in terms of LTV, it is further necessary to divide treatments of LTV that are really veiled versions of the labor theory of property from treatments that are focused on value theory as a quasi-price theory.

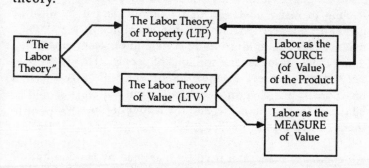

Figure 1.1 "The Labor Theory"

The property-oriented versions emphasize labor as the *source* or *cause* of (the value of) the product, while the price-oriented versions consider labor as the *measure* of value. The thick arrow from the "Labor as the SOURCE (of Value) of the Product" box back to the "labor theory of property" box indicates that (as will be explained below) the source-versions of LTV are essentially veiled versions of LTP.

Is Labor Peculiar?

It is remarkable that the human science of "Economics" has not been able to find or recognize any fundamental difference between the actions of human beings (i.e. "labor") and the services of things (e.g. the services of the widget-maker machine). Neoclassical economics uses two pictures of the production process—an *"active" poetical picture* and a *passive engineering picture*—both of which view labor as being symmetrical with the services of things.

The poetic view animistically pictures land and capital as "agents of productions" that (who?) cooperate together with workers to produce the product. Land is the mother and labor is the father of the harvest. This personification of land and capital is an example of the *pathetic fallacy*. It has long been criticized by radical economists such as Thomas Hodgskin:

> ...the language commonly in use is so palpably wrong, leading to many mistakes, that I cannot pass it by altogether in silence. We speak, for example, in a vague manner, of a windmill grinding corn, and of steam engines doing the work of several millions of people. This gives a very incorrect view of the phenomena. It is not the instruments which grind corn, and spin cotton, but the labour of those who make, and the labour of those who use them... . (Hodgskin, 1827, pp. 250–1)

> All capital is made and used by man; and by leaving him out of view, and ascribing productive power to capital, we take that as the active cause, which is only the creature

18

of his ingenuity, and the passive servant of his will. (Hodgskin, 1827, p. 247; quoted in King, 1983, p. 355)

For instance, the name "widget-maker" pictures the machine as making widgets. Marx was later to ridicule the same animism in capitalist economics.

It is an enchanted, perverted, topsy-turvy world, in which Monsieur le Capital and Madame la Terre do their ghost-walking as social characters... . (Marx, 1967, p. 830)

This *active poetic view* can be represented as follows.

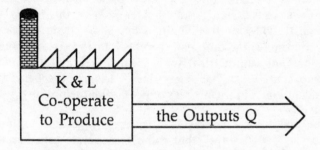

Figure 1.2 The Active Poetic View of Production

The other view favored in capitalist economics (particularly in technical contexts) is the *passive engineering view*. Human actions are treated simply as causally efficacious services of workers alongside the services of land and capital.

The engineering view switches to the passive voice: "Given input K and L, the outputs Q are produced."

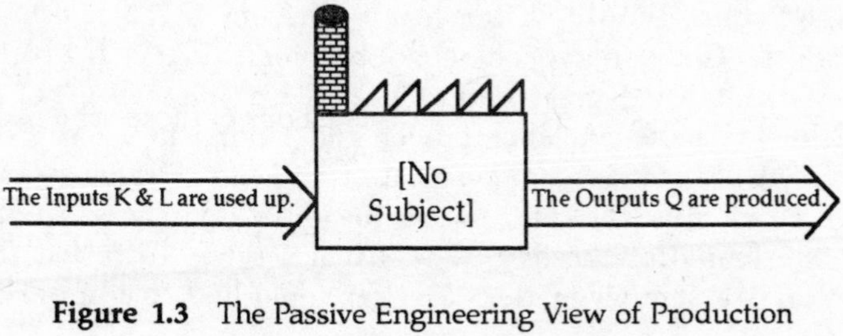

Figure 1.3 The Passive Engineering View of Production

In technical presentations, a production process is represented by a production function, $y = f(x_1, x_2, ..., x_n)$, meaning that given the inputs $x_1, x_2, ..., x_n$, the outputs y are produced. The notation usually does not distinguish between the "labor inputs" and the other inputs. The question "Produced by who?" is off-limits because the "who" (the workers of the enterprise) has been reconceptualized as just another input, the labor input, in an engineering description of the production process. There is no active agent who uses up the inputs to produce the outputs. Production is pictured as a technological process that just takes place.

There is a third view, the *humanistic view* of production. Neo-classical economics does not emphasize this view. The humanistic view portrays human beings as using capital and land to produce the outputs. It treats human beings as persons who are not symmetrical with things like capital and land. Human actions, or "labor services," use up the services of capital and land in the process of producing the product.

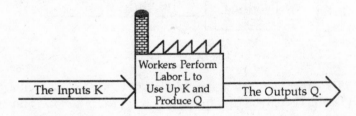

Figure 1.4 The Humanistic View of Production

Radical economists have also attempted to find a unique and relevant characteristic of labor ("Only labor is the source of value") that would differentiate it from the other factor services. These attempts have not been particularly fruitful.

Marx attached great importance to his "discovery" of the distinction between labor power and labor time. Yet that distinction is not even unique to labor. When one rents a car for a day, one buys the right to use the car ("car power") within certain limits for the day. The actual services extracted from the car are another matter. The car could be left in a parking

20

lot, or driven continuously at high speeds. To prevent being "exploited" by heavy users of "car time," car rental companies typically charge not just a flat day rate but have also a "piece-rate" based on the intensity of use as measured by mileage.

The labor-power/labor-time distinction gets heavy play in literary presentations of Marxian exploitation theory. That distinction, aside from being non-unique to labor, plays no role whatsoever in the modern mathematical development of the Marxian labor theory of value and exploitation using input-output theory (see Ellerman, 1983). There "is in fact no place in the formal analysis at which the labor/labor power distinction gets introduced" (Wolff, 1984, 178). But the relevant point here is that the development of the whole labor theory of value and exploitation is not based on any unique property of labor. One could just as well develop (say) a theory of corn value which would show how corn is "exploited" in a productive economy (see Wolff, 1984).

Thus we have the twofold situation wherein conventional economics does not recognize any fundamental and relevant differentiation of the actions of human beings from the services of things, while Marxian economics tries to isolate a unique and relevant property of labor (labor time versus labor power) as a basis for its theory of value and exploitation—but it fails to do so successfully.

Marx touched on deeper themes when he differentiated human labor from the services of the lower animals (and things) in his description of the labor process.

We presuppose labour in a form in which it is an exclusively human characteristic. A spider conducts operations which resemble those of the weaver, and a bee would put many a human architect to shame by the construction of its honeycomb cells. But what distinguishes the worst architect from the best of bees is that the architect builds the cell in his mind before he constructs it in wax. At the end of every labour process, a result emerges which had already been conceived by the worker at the beginning, hence already existed ideally. (Marx, 1977, pp. 283–4)

This conscious directedness and purposefulness of human action is part of what is now called the *intentionality* of human action (see Searle, 1983). This characterization does have significant import, but Marx failed to connect intentionality to his labor theory of value and exploitation (or even to his labor-power/labor-time distinction). This is in part because Marx tried to develop a labor theory of value as opposed to a labor theory of property.

Only Labor is Responsible

If we move from the artificially delimited field of "economics" into the adjacent field of law and jurisprudence, then it is easy to recognize a fundamental and unique characteristic of labor. *Only labor can be responsible.* The responsibility for events may not be imputed or charged against non-persons or things. The instruments of labor and the means of production can only serve as conductors of responsibility, never as the source.

> An instrument of labour is a thing, or a complex of things, which the worker interposes between himself and the object of his labour and which serves as a conductor, directing his activity onto that object. He makes use of the mechanical, physical and chemical properties of some substances in order to set them to work on other substances as instruments of his power, and in accordance with his purposes. (Marx, 1977, p. 285)

Marx did not *explicitly* use the concept of responsibility or cognate notions such as intentionality. After Marx died, the genetic code of Marxism was fixed. Any later attempt to introduce these notions was heresy.

While Marx did not use the word "responsibility," he nevertheless clearly describes the labor process as involving people as the uniquely responsible agents acting through things as mere *conductors* of responsibility. The responsibility for the results is imputed back through the instruments to the human agents using the instruments. Regardless of the "productivity" of the burglary tools (in the sense of causal efficacy), the responsibility for the burglary is imputed back through the tools solely to the burglar.

The natural sciences take no note of responsibility. The notion of responsibility (as opposed to causality) is not a concept of physics and engineering. The difference between the responsible actions of persons and the non-responsible services of things would not be revealed by a simple engineering description of the causal consequences of the actions/services. Therefore when economists choose to restrict their description of the production process to an engineering production function, they are implicitly or explicitly deciding to ignore the difference between the actions of persons and the services of things.

The various pictures of production—the active poetic view, the passive engineering view, and the humanistic view—can be illustrated by three possible confessions from George Washington after he used an axe to chop down the cherry tree.

— *Active Poetic View*: I cannot tell a lie; an axe cooperated with me to chop down the cherry tree.
— *Passive Engineering View*: I cannot tell a lie; given an axe and some of my labor, the cherry tree was chopped down.
— *Humanistic View*: I cannot tell a lie; I used an axe to chop down the cherry tree.

What is the difference? There is no difference from the viewpoint of the natural sciences. The difference concerns *responsibility*; each confession gives a different shading to the question of responsibility. The inability of capitalist economics to recognize that unique and relevant characteristic of labor is an ideological blindspot which reflects the symmetrical fact that both labor services and the services of land and capital are salable commodities in a capitalist economy. To analytically treat labor as being fundamentally different— when the capitalist system treats labor as a salable commodity like the services of capital and land—would be a perversity as abhorrent as preaching abolitionism in the middle of the Antebellum South.

Juridical Principle of Imputation = Labor Theory of Property

The pre-Marxian Ricardian socialists (or classical laborists) such as Proudhon, William Thompson, and Thomas Hodgskin tried to develop "the labor theory" as the labor theory of property. The most famous slogan of these classical laborists was "Labour's Claim to the whole product" (see Hodgskin, 1832 or Menger, 1899).

This claim was hindered by their failure to clearly include the liabilities for the used-up inputs in their concept of the "whole product." This allowed the orthodox caricature, "all the GNP would go to labor and none to property" (Samuelson, 1976, p. 626), *as if* there were no liabilities for the used-up inputs to be appropriated along with the produced outputs. If Labor appropriated the whole product, that would include appropriating the liabilities for the property used up in the production process in addition to appropriating the produced outputs. Present Labor would have to pay input suppliers (e.g. past Labor) to satisfy those liabilities.

The Ricardian socialists' development of the labor theory of property was also hindered by their failure to interpret the theory in terms of the juridical norm of legal imputation in accordance with (*de facto*) responsibility. LTP is concerned with responsibility in the ex post sense of the question "Who did it?", not with "responsibilities" in the ex ante sense of one's duties or tasks in an organizational role. A person or group of people are said to be *de facto or factually responsible* for a certain result if it was the purposeful result of their intentional (joint) actions. The assignment of *de jure or legal responsibility* is called "imputation." The basic *juridical principle of imputation* is that *de jure* or legal responsibility is to be imputed in accordance with *de facto* or factual responsibility. For example, the legal responsibility for a civil or criminal wrong should be assigned to the person or persons who intentionally committed the act, i.e. to the *de facto* responsible party.

In the context of assigning property rights and obligations, the juridical principle of imputation is expressed as the *labor theory of property* which holds that people should appropriate the (positive and negative) fruits of their labor. Since, in

24

the economic context, intentional human actions are called "labor," we can express the *equivalence* as:

The Juridical Principle of Imputation: =	*The Labor Theory of Property:*
People should have the legal responsibility for the positive and negative results of their intentional actions.	People should legally appropriate the positive and negative fruits of their labor.

In other words, the juridical principle of imputation is the labor theory of property applied in the context of civil and criminal trials, and the labor theory of property is the juridical principle applied in the context of property appropriation.

De facto responsibility is *not* a normative notion; it is a descriptive factual notion. The juridical principle of imputation is a normative principle which states that legal or de jure responsibility should be assigned in accordance with *de facto* responsibility. In the jury system, the jury is assigned the *factual question* of "officially" determining whether or not the accused party was *de facto* responsible for the deed as charged. If "Guilty" then legal responsibility is imputed accordingly.

Economics is always on "jury duty" to determine "the facts" about human activities. These are not value judgments (where social scientists have no particular expertise). The economist–as–juror is only required to make factual descriptive judgments about *de facto* responsibility. The normative and descriptive questions should be kept conceptually distinct. That separation is difficult since, given the juridical principle, *de facto* responsibility implies de jure responsibility.

In a given productive enterprise, the economist-as-juror faces the descriptive question of what or, rather, who is *de facto* responsible for producing the product by using up the various inputs? The *marginal productivity* of tools (machine tools or burglary tools) is not relevant to this factual question of *responsibility* either inside or outside the courtroom. Only human actions can be responsible; the services provided by things cannot be responsible (no matter how causally efficacious). The original question includes the question of who is responsible for using up those casually efficacious or productive services of the tools.

One of the original developers of marginal productivity theory in economics, Friedrich von Wieser, admitted that of all the factors of production, only labor is responsible.

> The judge,... who, in his narrowly-defined task, is only concerned with the legal imputation, confines himself to the discovery of the legally responsible factor,—that person, in fact, who is threatened with the legal punishment. On him will rightly be laid the whole burden of the consequences, although he could never by himself alone—without instruments and all the other conditions—have committed the crime. The imputation takes for granted physical causality.
> ... If it is the moral imputation that is in question, then certainly no one but the labourer could be named. Land and capital have no merit that they bring forth fruit; they are dead tools in the hand of man; and the man is responsible for the use he makes of them. (Wieser, 1930, pp. 76–9)

These are remarkable admissions. Wieser at last has in his hands the correct explanation of the old radical slogans "Only labor is creative" or "Only labor is productive," which even the classical laborists and Marxists could not explain clearly.

Wieser's response to his insights exemplifies what often passes for moral reasoning among many economists and social theorists in general. Any stable socio-economic system will provide the conditions for its own reproduction. The bulk of the people born and raised under the system will be appropriately educated so that the superiority of the system will be "intuitively obvious" to them. They will not use some purported abstract moral principle to evaluate the system; the system is "obviously" correct. Instead any moral principle is itself judged according to whether or not it supports the system. If the principle does not agree with the system, then "obviously" the principle is incorrect, irrelevant, or inapplicable.

The fact that only labor could be legally or morally responsible therefore did not lead Wieser to question capitalist appropriation. It only told him that the usual notions of responsibility and imputation were not "relevant" to capitalist

26

appropriation. Capitalist apologetics would require a new metaphorical notion of "economic imputation" in accordance with another new notion of "economic responsibility."

> In the division of the return from production, we have to deal similarly ... with an imputation,—save that it is from the economic, not the judicial point of view. (Wieser, 1930, p. 76)

By defining "economic responsibility" in terms of the animistic version of marginal productivity, Wieser could finally draw his desired conclusion that competitive capitalism "economically" imputes the product in accordance with "economic" responsibility.

In spite of Wieser's candid admission a century ago that "no one but the labourer could be named" and that the assignment of legal responsibility "takes for granted physical causality," the author has not been able to find a single contemporary economics text, elementary or advanced, which similarly admits that among all the causally efficacious factors, only labor is responsible. The legal system's treatment of "labor" as the only responsible "input service" is apparently a forbidden topic in economics. Contemporary texts cannot use the R-word. The same texts express their "puzzlement" at how so many earlier political economists could "overlook" land and capital, and believe that "labor was the only productive factor." A closer reading of Wieser, not to mention common sense, would suggest another interpretation of the "labor theory."

What is Labor's Product?

Given a group of apple trees, consider the human activity of Adam picking apples for an hour to produce a bushel of apples. The human activity of picking the apples for an hour is reconceptualized in economics as another "input," a man-hour of apple-picking labor, to the now subjectless production process. Given a group of apples trees and a man-hour of apple-picking labor as inputs, a bushel of apples is produced as the output. The question of *who* uses the inputs to produce the outputs has no answer because the actions of the people carrying out the process are construed as just another input in the engineering description of a technological input-output process.

Prior to conceptualizing the human activity of production as an "input" to a dehumanized technological conception of production, we could use two-component lists (or vectors),

(outputs, inputs).

The productive activities of all the people working in the given production example produce Q by using up K, so (Q, –K) is *Labor's product*. The labor L performed by the people working in the enterprise is simply a way to refer to the human activity of producing (Q, –K).

Labor L = Human Activity of Producing (Q, –K)

But then that activity L is reconceptualized as another "input," an input to the now subjectless production process. Using this artificial reconceptualization, the people working in the production process produce the labor services L and then use up K as well as L in the production of Q. Using the vector notation, they produce the labor (0, 0, L) and they produce the *whole product* (Q, –K, –L) which add together (by adding the corresponding components) to yield the three-component version of Labor's product.

Labor's product = (Q, –K, 0)   = (Q, –K, –L)   + (0, 0, L)
                               = whole product + labor services.

In capitalist production, the people working in the firm, i.e. the party herein called "Labor," appropriate and sell only their labor services to the employer who, in turn, appropriates the whole product. In a democratic firm, Labor appropriates Labor's product (which is the sum of the whole product and the labor services). The difference between the two forms of production lies in who appropriates the whole product which consists of the produced outputs Q and the liabilities –K and –L for the used-up inputs and labor activity. Under capitalist production, the workers still produce Labor's product (since that is a question of fact unchanged by the legal superstructure) but only appropriate their labor services as a commodity. Hence the assets and liabilities that they produce but do not appropriate constitute the whole product (subtract corresponding components in the lists).

$$
\begin{array}{ll}
\text{Labor's Product} & = (Q, -K, 0) \\
\text{Minus: Labor as a} & \\
\quad\text{Commodity} & = -(0, 0, L) \\
\hline
\text{Equals: Whole Product} & = (Q, -K, -L).
\end{array}
$$

In words, the equation is as follows.

What Labor Produces
Minus: What Labor Produces and Appropriates
Equals: What Labor Produces But Does Not Appropriate.

The labor theory of property holds that the people working in every enterprise should appropriate the positive and negative fruits of their labor which in the vector notation is Labor's product (= whole product + labor services). Thus in the comparison with the capitalist firm, the labor theory of property implies that Labor should appropriate the whole product. We saw before that "appropriating the whole product" was a property-oriented description of being the residual claimant, i.e. being the firm. In short, the labor theory of property implies that Labor should be the firm, i.e. that the firm should be a worker-owned firm.

It is important to understand what this argument does *not* imply. We have already taken some pains to separate the residual claimant's role from the capital-owner's role. The labor theory of property implies that Labor should have the residual claimant's role. It does not imply that the current workers in any enterprise should own the capital assets of that enterprise which have been accumulated from the past. The argument does imply that the current workers are *de facto* responsible for and should be legally responsible for using up the services of those capital assets (i.e. should be legally responsible for the input-liabilities –K).

Entrepreneurship

In presenting the labor theory of property, we have used the conventional economic representation of production where some product Q is produced by the workers performing the labor L using up the inputs K. It is a trite criticism of economic theory to point out that this oversimplifies and misrepresents reality. All theorizing involves some idealization and simplification in order to focus on the important structure and not be overwhelmed by irrelevant detail.

Some simplifications improve expositional clarity without sacrificing theoretical generality. For example, we have represented all the non-labor inputs as K units of capital services. But the theory applies just as well to enterprises which have any number of different kinds of non-labor inputs. The symbol K could be replaced by a vector or list $(K_1, K_2, ..., K_n)$ which could then represent a large number ("n") of different kinds of capital services, intermediate or semi-finished goods, and the services of land and natural resources. Similarly, Q and L could be replaced by vectors $(Q_1, Q_2, ..., Q_m)$ and $(L_1, L_2, ..., L_p)$ to represent different types of outputs (including services) and labor services.

There are limitations, however, to the representation of production as a given process of labor producing a set of outputs by using up a set of inputs. That representation neglects the set of factors grouped under the label "entrepreneurship."

Entrepreneurship requires special treatment since it does not take the production process as a "given." The entrepreneur or entrepreneurial group sets up and develops the productive organization wherein L uses up K to produce Q.

The acknowledged special nature of entrepreneurship, however, does not turn other less creative forms of human activity into the services of things. The system of business based on the employment relation treats human beings as entities which may be hired or rented. In capitalist ideology, the one form of labor that is exempted from this treatment is "entrepreneurship"—which is sometimes treated in the opposite fashion as the source of all responsibility for the results of production.

This repeats in a modern form one of the oldest forms of ideology to be found in history: the representation of one set of people as being supremely creative and responsible while another set of people are relatively thing-like. Ancient and Antebellum slavery offer obvious examples. The English revolutionary, Richard Rumbold, and later Thomas Jefferson criticized this ideology as the view that "some are born with saddles on their backs ready to be ridden, while others are born booted and spurred, ready to ride." The emphasis is not on "born." The critique is of any society which partitions people into two groups (based on birth or on meritocratic achievements), with one group or class treated essentially as things while the other is supremely human.

The Chicago school of economics emphasizes the updated form of this ancient ideology. Humanity is partitioned into "risk-takers" and "risk-averters."

> This fact is responsible for the most fundamental change of all in the form of organization, the system under which the confident and venturesome "assume the risk" and "insure" the doubtful and timid by guaranteeing to the latter a specified income in return for an assignment of the actual results...The result of this manifold specialization of function is *enterprise and the wage system of industry.* (Knight, 1965, pp. 269–71)

The Austrian school of economics (which finds its vulgar reflection in the Ayn Rand-type literature) goes to even greater extremes celebrating the risk-taking entrepreneurs—as if they were *ubermensch* compared to which lesser humans were thing-like.

31

Capitalist ideology has been given something of a "free ride" by having Marxian socialism as the acknowledged alternative. This has allowed the employment system ("capitalism") to be associated with a number of principles that it in fact violates (but less so than Marxism). Capitalism is associated with private property, but we have seen in this chapter that the employment relation inherently denies people the right to the fruits of their labor—which is widely, if not universally, acknowledged as the best foundation for the right of private ownership. Capitalism is also associated with democracy. Yet as we will see in the next chapter, the employment contract is essentially a scaled-down version of the Hobbes' anti-democratic pact of subjugation wherein people give up and alienate the right to govern themselves to a sovereign (the employer is *not* the representative or delegate of the employees).

In a similar manner, capitalism is associated with entrepreneurship. But that is not an entirely happy marriage. Entrepreneurship is a form of labor, not a form of capital. Within the employment system, the conflict is most acute when entrepreneurs negotiate with venture capitalists for control of the enterprise. It is an old tale how entrepreneurs may team up with venture capitalists and end up as hired managers or as being unemployed since the control rights to the conventional corporation are attached to the ownership of the capital shares.

The great benefit of the employment system for entrepreneurs is not what it allows venture capitalists to do to them, but what it allows entrepreneurs to do to everyone else working in the enterprise. Assuming access to adequate capital, the employment contract allows the entrepreneur to employ, hire, or rent (i.e. humanly "leverage") everyone else involved in the firm so that he or she alone has the control and residual rights. From the legal viewpoint, the *de facto* responsible actions of all the others involved in the venture are treated as thing-like services.

In a democratic firm, there is no assumption that everyone's work is of equal value to the enterprise. Entrepreneurial work is the most creative and often the most important form of work in an enterprise. Without it, the enterprise would not have been organized.

In a similar manner, political revolutionaries may play an indispensable entrepreneurial role in setting up a democratic polity. But that does not mean that the revolutionary leaders should "own" the polity as their kingdom—although many will try (human nature being what it is). It has often been said that George Washington's most important contribution to American democracy was leaving office peacefully. It is possible to recognize the contribution of a leader and revolutionary without making him or her into a king or queen and without reducing everyone else to a subject.

The same should be possible in a democratic workplace. We have no algorithm for evaluating the entrepreneur's contribution. New legal mechanisms may be needed to recognize the entrepreneur's role—new mechanisms that do not treat everyone else in the firm as a rented resource. The entrepreneur's product is often intangible, a form of intellectual property or an organizational structure. In the capitalist milieu, it may be captured not as a form of intellectual property but as ownership of the corporation. In a democratic milieu, corporations are not owned as property so it is necessary to use more accurate and refined forms of property (e.g. intellectual property in the form of patents and copyrights) to capture the entrepreneur's contribution. For instance, an entrepreneur might develop a new product and then set up a democratic firm to produce it. Instead of having "ownership" of the company, the entrepreneur would receive a royalty payment for each unit sold in addition to the salary received as an entrepreneur-manager.

In this manner, the contribution of the entrepreneur can be recognized and valued without reducing the other people working in the enterprise to the role of rented resources. No doubt, all such arrangements would have the "flaw" that they would not give the entrepreneur the *same* wealth and power as would "ownership of the corporation." In the same manner, political democracy suffers from the flaw that it does not afford political revolutionaries the same wealth and unaccountable power as would some form of dictatorship—which is why so many revolutionaries opt for the latter.

Property Theoretic Themes in Marxian Value Theory

We turn now to the task of intellectual reclamation—trying to salvage some of Marx's "labor theory"—a task that is little appreciated by both conventional and Marxist economists. Marx's labor theory of value—as a theory to measure value—is one of the most spectacular failures in the history of economic thought (see Ellerman, 1983 for analysis and criticism). There is, however, the alternative interpretation of Marx's theory which emphasizes labor-as-source instead of labor-as-measure. That turns out to be a disguised version of the labor theory of property, not a value theory at all. In this section, we try to tease out these property-theoretic themes in Marxian thought.

Marx started by singling out human action as the unique activity that acted upon the world to endow it with intents and purposes—even though Marx and latter-day Marxists do not use the notion of responsibility to differentiate human actions from the services of things (Marxists have been as unable as capitalist economists to find the R-word).

> But although part of Nature and subject to the determinism of natural laws, Man as a conscious being had the distinctive capability of struggling with and against Nature—of subordinating and ultimately transforming it for his own purposes. This was the unique rôle of human productive activity, or human labour, which differentiated man from all (or nearly all) other animate creatures ... (Dobb, 1973, pp. 143–4)

Marx clearly saw that physical causal processes can never be co-responsible with human agents; the causal processes serve only as "conductors" to transmit human intentions. Hence the assignment of legal responsibility in accordance with *de facto* responsibility "takes for granted physical causality."

Marx also was by no means exclusively concerned with developing the labor-as-a-measure version of LTV. It was not simply that value is a function of labor, but that direct labor *creates* the value added to the material inputs.

34

For the capitalist, the selling price of the commodities produced by the worker is divided into three parts: *first*, the replacement of the price of the raw materials advanced by him together with replacement of the depreciation of the tools, machinery and other means of labour also advanced by him; *secondly*, the replacement of the wages advanced by him, and *thirdly*, the surplus left over, the capitalist's profit. While the first part only replaces *previously existing values*, it is clear that both the replacement of the wages and also the surplus profit of the capitalist are, on the whole, taken from the *new value created by the worker's labour* and added to the raw materials. (Marx, 1972, p. 182)

We previously drew a conceptual road map of "The Labor Theory" which saw it divide into LTP and LTV. Then LTV divided into "labor as source" and "labor as measure" theories. The source versions of LTV are best understood as (confused) value-theoretic renditions of the labor theory of property.

The source/measure dichotomy should not be confused with a prescriptive-descriptive dichotomy. "Responsibility for" (or "source of") has a descriptive (*de facto*) and a normative (de jure) interpretation. The descriptive question of who is *de facto* responsible for committing a burglary is distinct from the normative question of who should be held de jure responsible for the burglary. The imputation principle—that de jure responsibility should be assigned according to *de facto* responsibility—provides the link between the two questions.

The source version of LTV and LTP also have both a descriptive and a prescriptive side. The controversy lies largely on the descriptive side although the normative parts are necessary to complete any critique of capitalist production. The descriptive side of neo-classical economics (e.g. marginal productivity theory) resorts to metaphor (pathetic fallacy) to picture causality as "responsibility"—to picture each causally efficacious factor as being responsible for producing a share of the product.

Classical laborists, such as Thomas Hodgskin, as well as Marx criticized this personification of the factors. They based the source-LTV and LTP on the unique attribute of labor that it is the only "creative" factor. That attribute of *de facto* responsibility is not a concept of the natural sciences. But it is central to the descriptive side of the source-LTV.

> The crucial descriptive aspect remains the capturing of the human dimension of production and distribution in the labour theory of value viewed as a category of descriptive statements, rather than the possibility of "determining" or "predicting" prices on the basis of values,... (Sen, 1978, p. 183)

Economists who seem to take as their professional mission to rationalize an economy that treats persons as things (by allowing them to be hired or rented), may well tend to adopt the science of things (physics and other natural sciences) as the scientific model for "economics." Attempts to use notions unique to the human sciences—such as the notions of "responsibility" or "intentionality"—to differentiate labor from the services of things are thus deemed inappropriate in the "science" of economics.

Marx did take labor as the unique source of the value-added so Marx played both sides of the source/measure dichotomy. It was not simply that direct labor was a measure of the value of the surplus product but that direct labor was the *source* of the surplus product. Indeed, Marx's whole exploitation analysis only makes sense under the labor-as-source interpretation of the labor theory of value. The point was *not* that labor created *the value of* the product, but that labor *created the product itself*.

> And it is this fairly obvious truth which, I contend, lies at the heart of the Marxist charge of exploitation. The real basis of that charge is not that workers produce value, but that they produce what has it. (Cohen, 1981, p. 219)

In the assertion that "labor created *the value of* the product," the phrase "the value of" can be deleted and thrown, along with the measure-LTV, into the dustbin of intellectual history.

Some economists have been quite explicit about the (non-orthodox) property-theoretic interpretation of Marx's value theory. Thorstein Veblen was never a slave to the standard or

36

orthodox interpretation of any theory. Veblen saw natural rights arguments standing behind the general thrust of Marx's theory. Veblen sees the claim of Labor's right to the whole product implicit in Marx and traces it to the classical laborists or Ricardian socialists.

> Chief among these doctrines, in the apprehension of his critics, is the theory of value, with its corollaries: (a) the doctrines of the exploitation of labor by capital; and (b) the laborer's claim to the whole product of his labor. Avowedly, Marx traces his doctrine of labor value to Ricardo, and through him to the classical economists. The laborer's claim to the whole product of labor, which is pretty constantly implied, though not frequently avowed by Marx, he has in all probability taken from English writers of the early nineteenth century, more particularly from William Thompson. (Veblen, 1952, p. 316)

Recent scholarship would, however, emphasize the influence on Marx of Hodgskin and Bray more than Thompson (see King, 1983 and Henderson, 1985).

Gunnar Myrdal finds a similar reason behind even Ricardo's use of labor as the basis for his value theory in spite of criticism from Malthus, Say, and Bentham.

> The solution of this puzzle may be found in the natural law notion that property has its natural justification in the labour bestowed on an object. (Myrdal, 1969, p. 70)

But the implications of the labor theory inevitably conflict with classical liberalism which fully accepted wage labor. The foundation of the theory is the uniqueness of labor; of all the causally efficacious factors, labor is the only responsible agent.

> Man alone is alive, nature is dead; human work alone creates values, nature is passive. Man alone is *cause*, as Rodbertus said later, whilst external nature is only a set of *conditions*. Human work is the only active cause which is capable of creating value. This is also the origin of the

37

concept "productive factor". It is not surprising that the classics recognized only *one* productive factor, viz., labour. The same metaphysical analogies that were used to establish natural rights were also used to expound the idea of natural or real value. It is an example of the previously mentioned attempt of the philosophy of natural law to derive both rights and value from the same ultimate principles. (Myrdal, 1969, p. 72)

Thus the Janus-headed "labor theory" has long served as both a property theory and a value theory—even though orthodox economists only *want* to see it as a (fallacious) price theory in Marx.

They tend to focus attention on the theory of exchange value [and] neglect its foundations ... Marx was right in saying that his surplus value theory follows from the classical theory of real value, admittedly with additions from other sources. Moreover, Marx was not the first to draw radical conclusions from it. All pre-Marxist British socialists derived their arguments from Adam Smith and later from Ricardo. (Myrdal, 1969, p. 78)

It is time to step back for a moment and consider Marx's value theory in a larger context.

[T]he "naturalness" of labour as the moral title to what is created by that labour has been a commonplace of political and economic radicalism for three hundred years; and political and economic conservatism has had a continuous struggle to defuse the revolutionary implications of it. (Ryan, 1984, p. 1)

The central point of the labour theory as a theory of exploitation is that *labour is the only human contribution to economic activity, and the exercise of labour power should be the only way in which a claim to the net product of a nonexploitative economic system is acquired.* (Nuti, 1977, p. 96)

A typical response by Marxists is "None of this, by the way, implies that Marx intended the labor theory of value as a theory of property rights, à la Locke or even Proudhon," (Shaikh, 1977, p. 121) as if the question of what "Marx intended" was relevant beyond the confines of Marxology.

The Employment Contract vs. *de facto* Inalienability

"Private ownership of the means of production" is not the culprit. We have seen enough of the plot to ferret out the true villain of the piece. The labor theory of property normatively implies that Labor (the workers including managers) in each enterprise ought to be the residual claimant for that enterprise. We previously noted the descriptive fact that any legal party could be the residual claimant by becoming the hiring party, the party who hires (or already owns) all the inputs to be used up in production. The workers' claim to the positive and negative fruits of their labor is thus legally defeated by the workers being hired, i.e. by the employment contract. It is thus the employment contract that defeats the legal implementation of the labor theory of property.

The employer–employee contract inherently conflicts with people's right to the fruits of their labor. The employment contract is the contract for the voluntary hiring or renting of human beings. When a person is legally rented or "employed," then the person has no legal responsibility for the positive or negative results of his or her actions; that legal responsibility goes to the employer. Renting capital gives financial leverage ("gearing" in the UK); it multiplies the effect of the equity capital. Similarly, renting people creates *human leverage*; it multiplies the effect of the employer—*as if* all the results were the fruits of solely the employer's labor.

This conflict between "employment" and *de facto* responsibility has long been apparent in the law. We noted previously that the labor theory of property was only a property-theoretic rendition of the usual juridical principle of imputing legal responsibility in accordance with *de facto* responsibility. We also saw that—unlike the services of things—the actions of persons are *de facto* responsible. That *de facto* responsibility is independent of legal contracts, i.e. people do not suddenly become non-responsible tools or instruments when they sign an employment contract. The legal authorities only explicitly apply the juridical principle when a human activity ends up in court, i.e. when a criminal or civil wrong has been committed. When an employee—even within the context of a normal employment relation—commits a crime at the behest of the employer, then the employee suddenly becomes a partner in the enterprise.

> All who participate in a crime with a guilty intent are liable to punishment. A master and servant who so participate in a crime are liable criminally, not because they are master and servant, but because they jointly carried out a criminal venture and are both criminous. (Batt, 1967, p. 612)

The legal authorities will not allow an employment contract to be used by an employee to avoid the legal responsibility for his or her *de facto* responsible actions.

But when the "venture" being "jointly carried out" is a normal capitalist enterprise, the workers do not suddenly become *de facto* non-responsible tools or instruments. They are just as much *de facto* responsible together with the working employer as when "they jointly carried out a criminal venture." It is the reaction of the law that suddenly changes. Now the employment contract for the renting of human beings is accepted as a "valid" contract. The *de facto* responsibility of human action is nevertheless not factually transferable even though the legal authorities now accept the employment contract for the sale of labor as a commodity as "valid."

The legal system faced the same internal contradiction when it treated slaves as legal chattel in the Antebellum South. The legally non-responsible instrument in work suddenly became a responsible person when committing a crime.

> The slave, who is but "*a chattel*" on all *other* occasions, with not one solitary attribute of personality accorded to him, becomes "*a person*" whenever he is to be *punished*. (Goodell, 1969, p. 309)

40

As an Antebellum Alabama judge put it, the slaves in fact

> are rational beings, they are capable of committing crimes; and in reference to acts which are crimes, are regarded as persons. Because they are slaves, they are ... incapable of performing civil acts, and, in reference to all such, they are things, not persons. (Catterall, 1926, p. 247)

It should be no surprise that the legal system involves the same contradiction when workers are rented instead of being owned. The rental relation is voluntary (unlike traditional slavery) but *de facto* responsibility is not voluntarily transferable. A person would not become a *de facto* non-responsible entity if he or she voluntarily agreed to the legal condition of slavery. And the hired criminal would certainly voluntarily agree to give up any and all responsibility for the results of his actions. But regardless of the language on the contract and regardless of the reaction of the legal system, the fact is that he remains a *de facto* responsible person.

It is useful in this connection to consider the *de facto* alienability of things. We *can* voluntarily give up and transfer the temporary use of a tool or instrument to another person so the other person can employ it and be solely *de facto* responsible for the results of that employment. The legal contract that fits the transfer is the lease or rental contract; the owner of the instrument rents, leases, or hires out the instrument to be used by someone else. The same facts do *not* apply to our *selves*. We cannot voluntarily give up and transfer the temporary use of our own persons to another person so the other person can "employ" us and be solely *de facto* responsible for the results of that employment. Our own *de facto* responsibility intrudes. From the factual viewpoint, we are inexorably partners. The so-called "employees" can only co-operate together with the worker employer but then they are jointly *de facto* responsible for the venture they "jointly carried out." But the law still treats the legal contract for the hiring of human beings as a "valid" contract even though human actions are not *de facto* transferable like the services of a tool or instrument.

41

The nice word for this is "legal fiction." The law will accept the *de facto* responsible co-operation of the "employees" *as if* that fulfilled the hiring contract. Or, at least, the law will do that if no crime has been committed. If a crime has been committed, then the law will not allow the labor theory of property (i.e. the juridical principle of imputation) to be defeated by the employment contract. The law will not allow this "fictional" transfer of labor to shield the criminous servant from legal responsibility. Then the fiction is set aside in favor of the facts; the enterprise is legally reconstructed as a partnership of all who worked in it.

The not-so-nice word for this is "fraud." When the legal system "validates" the contract for the renting of human beings, that is a fraud perpetrated on an institutional scale. It is our own peculiar institution.

This argument is an application to the employment contract of the *de facto theory of inalienable rights* that descends from the history of anti-slavery and democratic thought (see Ellerman, 1986a or 1989b). *De facto* responsibility is factually inalienable, and thus without having a legalized form of fraud, it must be legally inalienable. The legal contract to alienate and transfer that which is *de facto* inalienable is inherently invalid. The natural-law invalidity of the voluntary self-enslavement contract (to sell all of one's labor) is already legally recognized; the invalidity of the contract to rent or hire human beings should be similarly legally recognized.

The chapter began with an analysis of the Fundamental Myth of capitalism, that the residual claimant's role was part of the property rights of "ownership of the means of production." A frequent reply is that while it is "formally" true that residual claimancy is not part of capital ownership, the bargaining power of capital ownership is sufficient that "Capital hires Labor" at will. Thus residual claimancy is said to be *"in effect* part of the ownership of capital."

The rejoinder is that we are not arguing that the determination of the hiring party should be left to marketplace bargaining power (any more than the question of the ownership of human beings should be left to market transactions). The argument for the invalidity of the hired-labor contract completes the argument. With the contract for the renting of human beings ruled out as invalid, it would not be a question of bargaining power. All industry would be organized on the basis of people renting (or already owning) capital instead of the owners of capital renting people. Thus the capital suppliers— as capital suppliers—are denied the residual claimant's role (they might also work and be part of the residual claimant in that role). Since the residual claimant's role was never part of their property rights, this is no violation of their actual (as opposed to imagined) property rights. They are only denied the "freedom" to make the naturally invalid contract to rent other human beings.

There is no need to "adopt" the labor theory of property; it is already adopted. It is the fundamental juridical principle of imputation. Our argument is to "dis-adopt" the inherently invalid contract for the renting of human beings—the contract that defeats the application of the labor theory of property (when no crime has been committed). The facts of human responsibility are the same whether the venture is criminal or not. Every enterprise should be legally reconstructed as a partnership of all who work in the enterprise. Every enterprise should be a democratic worker-owned firm.

2
Democratic Theory

Democracy in the Firm

The Enterprise as a Governance Institution

Is a company an organization for the governance of people or only for the administration of things? If a company carries out any productive or service operations, then the people conducting those operations are governed by the company within the scope of those operations.

As a legal technicality, there could be an "uninhabited corporation" that served only a holding bin for assets that stood idle or were leased out to other companies or individuals. No one would *work* in such an "uninhabited company"; the shareholders would then only be concerned with "the administration of things."

Any company with people *working* in it is an institution of governance—so the question of democracy arises.

Stakeholders: the Governed and the Affected

Democracy is a structure for the governance of people, not the management of property. It is the structure wherein those who govern are selected by, and govern as the representatives of, the governed. In an economic enterprise, the managers are those who govern, but who are "the governed"?

The *stakeholders* in an enterprise are all those people who are either governed by the enterprise management or whose interests are affected by the enterprise. Thus the stakeholders would include:

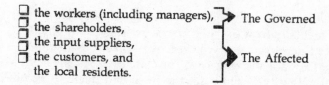

Figure 2.1 Stakeholders

But there is a crucial partition of this broad group of stake-holders into two groups which will be called "the governed" and "the affected."

"The governed" are those who (within certain limits) take orders from the enterprise management, i.e. who are under the authority of the managers.

"The affected" are those whose person or property are *only* affected by the activity of the enterprise but who are not personally under the authority of the management.

The shareholders are not under the authority of managers; neither are the suppliers of the material inputs, the customers, nor those who live in the vicinity of the enterprise's operations. All those people might have their interests affected by the activities of the firm, but they don't take orders from the firm. The workers do. Only the people who work in the firm are "the governed."

The employment system promotes the mental acrobatics of dividing a person into two different legal roles: (1) the owner and seller of labor services (the labor-seller role), and (2) the person who performs the labor services (the worker role). Under slavery, different people might play the two roles as when a master hired out some of his slaves to work for someone else during slack times. In modern times, there has even developed a labor resale market—called "employee leasing"—which separates the two roles. A person rents himself or herself to company A and then company A rents or leases the person to company B. In the second labor-sale contract, the legal party selling the labor services (company A) is distinct from the person performing the labor.

In the normal capitalist firm, the employee plays both roles. Economists are fond of only considering the employee in his or her labor-seller role—just another input supplier. Then they can mentally treat the workers as external input suppliers who indeed do have direct control over their labor-selling activities. They are not "governed" *in that role*. Management has no legal authority to tell them the price and quantity involved in their labor-selling decision. It is in the employee's worker role that the person is governed by management, *not* in the employee's labor-seller role.

Direct versus Indirect Control

Discussions of corporate governance are often clouded by insufficient attention to the distinction between those who are governed by the corporation and those whose interests are only affected by the firm. Vague statements are made about all the stakeholders having the right to "control" the company to protect their affected interests. But such broad assertions about "control rights" are not too helpful since the control rights legally held by shareholders are fundamentally different from the control rights held by, say, suppliers and customers. In particular, there is a basic distinction between direct control rights (positive decision-making rights) and indirect control rights (negative decision-constraining rights) that should run parallel to the earlier distinction between the governed and those only affected by an enterprise.

We are discussing the decisions of a given enterprise, not the decisions of outside parties. The direct control rights are the rights to ultimately make the decisions of the enterprise. The managers make day-to-day decisions but they do so as the representatives of those who ultimately hold the direct control rights. In a conventional capitalist corporation, the common stockholders hold those direct control rights.

Outside parties, such as supplier or customers, have the direct control rights over their own decisions, but—relative to the enterprise's decisions—they have only an indirect or negative decision-constraining role. "No, I will not sell the firm these inputs at that price." "No, I will not buy that output on those terms." Even the worker in his or her labor-seller role can say "No, I will not sell that amount of labor at that price without this benefit."

46

The Affected Interests Principle

Those who are potentially affected by the operations of the enterprise should have an effective means to exert indirect control on the enterprise operations to protect their legitimate interests. This could be stated as the:

AFFECTED INTERESTS PRINCIPLE. Everyone whose rightful interests are affected by an organization's decisions should have a right of indirect control (e.g. a collective or perhaps individual veto) to constrain those decisions.

It is difficult to effectively implement this principle. The market is the customary means of protecting outside interests in a market economy. But even then, there are a host of externalities where outside interests are affected without the benediction of a market relationship. And within market relations, there could be monopolistic power on one side of the market so that there is "consent" but little choice. Or there could be such large informational asymmetries that "consent" is not meaningfully informed. In such cases, the government often intervenes to regulate the market and attempt to offer better protection of the affected interests. These acknowledged difficulties in the implementation of the affected interests principle need not detain us here. Our concern is the assignment of the direct control rights over the enterprise.

There is a related argument that should be mentioned. Pressure groups for particular sets of affected interests (e.g. consumers) sometimes argue that they should have voting seats on the corporate board of directors to protect their interests. Leaving aside the fallacious assumption that the role of the board should be to protect *outside* affected interests, it is nevertheless difficult to see how this tactic can work. It runs up against the "law of one majority"; each different and opposing group of external affected interests cannot have a majority on the board of directors. A minority board position may have some informational value but the vote then has little control value. To protect their affected interests, the minority outside interests must fall back on indirect control rights (e.g. negative covenants in market contracts or government regulations) which they had independently of the voting board seats.

The board of directors is the locus for the exercise of direct decision-making control rights, whereas the affected interests principle is only concerned with assigning indirect decision-constraining rights to the outside affected interests. The assignation of the direct control rights requires another principle, the democratic principle.

The Democratic Principle

Who ought to have the ultimate direct control rights over the decisions of the enterprise? Democracy gives an unequivocal answer: *the governed.*

THE DEMOCRATIC PRINCIPLE. The direct control
   rights over an organization should be assigned to the
   people who are governed by the organization so that
   they will then be self-governing.

The shareholders, suppliers, customers, and local residents are not under the authority of the enterprise; they are not the governed. Only the people working in the enterprise (in their worker role) are "the governed" so only they would be assigned the ultimate direct control rights by the democratic principle. Needless to say, the same person can have several functional roles, e.g. as worker, as consumer, or as capital supplier. The democratic principle would assign direct control rights to the person qua worker in the enterprise, not *qua* consumer or *qua* capital-supplier.

Self-determination within a democratic framework does not include the right to violate the rights of outsiders. A democratically governed township does not have the right to do what it wants to neighboring towns. Direct control rights are to be exercised within the constraints established by the indirect control rights of the external affected interests. In that manner, each group can be self-governing. The workers can self-manage their work and the consumers can self-manage their consumption—with each abiding by the constraints established by the other and with neither having direct control rights over the other.

"Shareholders' Democracy"

In a capitalist corporation, the shareholders (absentee or not) have ultimate direct control rights over the operations of the corporation. They are the "citizens" who exercise these control rights by electing the corporate directors, the "legislators," who are supposed to act as the representatives of and in the interests of the shareholder-citizens.

> The analogy between state and corporation has been congenial to American lawmakers, legislative and judicial. The shareholders were the electorate, the directors the legislature, enacting general policies and committing them to the officers for execution. (Chayes, 1966, p. 39)

The board of directors selects the top managers who, in turn, select the remainder of the management team that manages the day-to-day operations of the corporation.

The direct control rights of shareholders are more nominal than effective in the large corporations with publicly traded shares—as was pointed out long ago by Adolf Berle and Gardner Means (1967 [1932]). Public stock markets have effectively disenfranchised the common stockholders. Each shareholder has a miniscule amount of the vote, and huge transaction costs block the self-organization of shareholders into "parties." Most investors buy shares for the investment potential; the voting rights are only a vestigial attachment.

This "separation of ownership and control" creates a problem of legitimacy—legitimacy by *capitalist* standards. Corporate reformers dream of "real shareholders' democracy" wherein the shareholders effectively exercise their control rights. The difficulty in this call for "democracy" is that the shareholders never were "the governed."

> Shareholder democracy, so-called, is misconceived because the shareholders are not the governed of the

corporation whose consent must be sought. (Chayes, 1966, p. 40)

Perhaps an analogy is appropriate. A set of shareholders in England start off voting to elect the government of the American Colonies. Then their voting rights fall into disrepair so the autocratic government of the Colonies rules as a self-perpetuating oligarchy that is not answerable to the English shareholders (not to mention the American people). How can democracy be restored to America? Not by re-establishing the direct control of the outside shareholders but by reassigning the direct control rights to the governed.

How do corporate lawyers and legislators manage to avoid these none-too-subtle points? One popular method is to think of the corporation solely as a piece of property to be administered, not as an organization for the management of people. But that image would only be accurate if the corporation was "uninhabited," if no one worked in the corporation.

It is the employment contract that turns the capitalist corporation-as-property into an organization of governance. That organization is not democratic in spite of the "consent of the governed" to the employment contract. The employees do not delegate the governance rights to the employer to govern as their representative. In the employment contract, the workers alienate and transfer their legal right to govern their activities "within the scope of the employment" to the employer. The employment contract is thus a limited work-place version of the Hobbesian *pactum subjectionis*. The argument for applying the democratic principle to the work-place is thus an argument which implies disallowing the employment contract just as we currently disallow any such Hobbesian contract to alienate democratic rights in the political sphere (for an extended analysis of the employment contract, see Ellerman, 1989b).

When the democratic principle is applied across the board, then workers would always be member-owners in the company where they work and never just employees. The employment relation would be replaced by the membership relation.

Democratic Socialism is not Democratic in the Enterprise

"Democratic socialism" refers to a political-economic system where the bulk of industry is state-owned and the state is a political democracy. Is a state-owned firm in a political democracy a democratic firm? For example, is the Post Office a democratic organization since the post office workers, as citizens, elect a President who appoints the Postmaster General? The answer is "No," but it is important to understand why such state-owned firms are undemocratic.

Democratic socialism is often criticized on grounds of scale. For instance, the workers in any one state-owned company are such a small portion of the total citizenry that they can have little real control over their enterprise. Hence democratic state-socialists become democratic municipal-socialists. If the enterprise was owned by the *local* government, then perhaps the workers would be less alienated. Or at least that seems to be the reasoning.

These practical problems in democratic socialism only veil the flaw in the theory of government ownership, regardless of whether the government is local or national. Citizenship in a democratic polity such as a municipality is based on having the functional role of residing within the jurisdiction of the polity, e.g. having legal residence in the municipality. Thus municipal socialism in effect assigns the ultimate direct control rights to the local residents. Membership in a democratic enterprise is based on a different functional role, that of working within the enterprise. So-called "democratic socialism" assigns the ultimate control rights over the enterprise to the wrong functional role (the role that defines political citizenship) so it is not even democratic in theory— much less in practice—in the enterprise.

The Public/Private Distinction in Democratic Theory

Personal Rights and Property Rights

A *personal right* is a right that attaches to an individual because the person satisfies some qualification such as playing a certain functional role. Examples include basic human rights where the qualification is simply that of being human, and political citizenship rights in a polity (e.g. municipality) where the functional role is that of residing within the polity. In contrast, a person does not have to satisfy any particular functional role to hold a property right. A property right can be acquired from a prior owner or it can be appropriated as an initial right.

Personal rights are not transferable; they may not be bought or sold. If a personal right (that was supposed to be attached to a functional role) was treated as being marketable, then the buyer might not have the qualifying functional role. And if the would-be buyer did have the functional role, he or she would not need to "buy" the right.

In America, a person might have several quite different types of voting rights:

— a citizen's political vote in a municipal, state, or federal election;
— a worker's vote in a union;
— a member's vote in a cooperative; or
— a shareholder's votes attached to conventional corporate shares.

Which rights are personal rights and which are property rights?

Personal rights can be easily distinguished from property rights by the *inheritability test*. Since personal rights attach to the person by virtue of fulfilling a certain role, those rights would be extinguished when the person dies. Property rights, however, would pass on to the person's estate and heirs. That is the contrast, for example, between the voting rights people have in a democratic organization (a polity, a union, or a cooperative) and the voting rights people have as shareholders in a capitalist corporation. Political voting rights are personal rights that are extinguished when the citizen dies whereas voting corporate stock passes to the person's heirs.

When the direct control rights over an organization are attached to a certain functional role (e.g. the role of being governed by the organization) then that control is "tied down" and attached in a non-transferable way to the set of people having that role. In contrast, the ultimate control rights over a capitalist corporation are property rights attached to the voting shares so that ownership can not only change "overnight," it can also become very concentrated in a few hands.

The ultra-capitalist ideal seems to be to have all rights as marketable property rights (see Nozick, 1974). Then society is like a ship with none of the cargo tied down. Even if the ship starts out with the cargo evenly distributed, any wave will start the cargo shifting to one side. Then the shifting weight will cause even more tilt—which in turn causes more cargo to shift to that side.

A similar social instability would result from having political voting rights as marketable property rights. Even with an equal initial distribution, one vote per person, any disturbance would result in some votes being bought and sold which begins the process of accumulation. Then the resulting political concentration would lead to capturing more wealth, more voting buying, and even more concentration. Soon most of the political votes and power would end up in a few hands. Democracy inherently avoids that sort of accumulation process by "tying down" the voting rights as personal rights attached to the functional role of being governed.

We have just this sort of instability in the economic sphere. Capitalism has structured the profit rights and control rights over corporations—where new wealth is created—as transferable property rights. The resulting instability has accordingly led to an incredibly lopsided distribution of wealth. By Federal Reserve data for 1983, 58 per cent of corporate stock owned by individuals is owned by the richest one per cent of households. The richest one-half per cent of households owns 46 per cent of that corporate stock. Similar statistics apply to the United Kingdom.

> The richest 1 per cent of the population own over half the company shares, and nearly two-thirds of the land. The richest 5 per cent own 80 per cent of the shares and 86 per cent of the land, according to the latest available figures. (McDonald, 1989, p. 10)

The system of economic democracy ties down the profit and control rights over each firm to the functional role of working in that firm. Since those membership rights are non-transferable and non-inheritable, they cannot become concentrated. Workers come to a democratic firm and eventually leave or retire. They keep as property the profits they earn while working in the firm (even if the profits are retained and paid back to them later), but their membership in the firm is a personal right they enjoy only when they work in the firm.

Quarantining Democracy in the Public Sphere

Since the political democratic revolutions of the eighteenth and nineteenth centuries, the government has been the main provider and guarantor of personal rights. Those who own significant property tend to want as much of society as possible to be organized on the basis of property rights, not personal rights. Hence they want "less government." Well-intended advocates of extending democratic rights to economic issues want "more government." This leads to "democratic socialism" where the government swallows the commanding heights of industry.

This "great debate" is ill-posed. It is based on a pair of false identifications: (1) that the sphere of government ("the public sphere") is the sole arena for personal rights, and (2) that the sphere of social life outside the government ("the private sphere") is solely based on private property rights. That is the traditional public/private distinction. Capitalism has used it to quarantine the democratic germ in the public sphere of government, and thus to keep the democratic germ out of industry. Instead of redefining those public/private identifications, democratic state-socialism compounds the error by holding that industry can only be democratized by being nationalized.

The rights to democratic self-determination will not remain forever quarantined in the sphere of government. It is an empirical fact of history that, as a result of the political democratic revolutions, the government was the first major organization in society to be switched over to treating its direct control rights (voting rights) as personal rights. There is otherwise no inherent relationship that restricts the idea of democratic self-determination to the political government. There are a host of other non-government organizations in society, corporations, universities, and a broad range of non-profit corporations, where people are also under an authority relation. The "unalienable rights" to democratic self-determination that we enjoy in the political sphere should not suddenly evaporate in the other spheres of life.

The democratic firm is a model of an organization that is democratic and yet is still "private" in the sense of being non-governmental. The membership rights in a democratic firm are personal rights assigned to the functional role of working in the firm.

Redefining "Social" to Recast the Public/Private Distinction

The old public/private distinction is supported by both capitalists and state-socialists. The former use it to argue that the idea of democracy is inapplicable to private industry, and the latter use it to argue that democracy can only come to industry by nationalizing it. But both arguments are incorrect, and the public/private distinction itself must be recast.

The word "private" is used in two senses: (1) "private" in the sense of being non-governmental, and (2) "private" in the sense of being based on private property. Let us drop the first meaning and retain the second. Similarly "public" is used in two senses: (1) "public" in the sense of being governmental, and (2) "public" in the sense of being based on personal rights. Let us use the second meaning and take it as the definition of "social" (instead of "public"). Thus we have:

Social Institution ◄——► Based on Personal Rights

Private Organization ◄——► Based on Property Rights.

Figure 2.2 Suggested Redefinitions

By these redefinitions, a democratic firm is a social institution (while still being "private" in the other sense of being not of the government), while a capitalist corporation is a private firm (not because it is also non-governmental but because it is based on property rights).

People-based versus Property-based Organizations

The inheritability test can be used to differentiate personal rights from property rights; personal rights are extinguished when a person dies while property rights are passed on to the heirs. The personal/property rights distinction can be used to classify organizations according to whether the membership rights such as the voting rights are personal or property rights. Consider the membership rights in the following organizations:

— democratic political communities (national, state, or local);
— democratic firms (e.g. worker cooperatives),
— trade unions;
— capitalist corporations; and
— condominium associations.

The membership rights in the first three organizational types are personal rights while the membership rights (also called "ownership rights") in the last two are property rights.

A condominium is an association for the partial co-ownership of housing units (often part of one structure such as an apartment building). The members are the unit-owners. Each unit-owner exclusively owns one or more units, and all the unit-owners through the association own the remaining property in common (e.g. the surrounding grounds). Each unit is assigned a certain percentage of the whole depending on its access to common resources and its drain on common expenses. A unit casts its percentage of the votes and pays that percentage of any common assessments.

A condominium and a capitalist corporation have the common feature that the membership rights are attached to property shares (the units in a condominium and the shares of stock in a corporation) which are owned by persons. In contrast, membership in the other three organizations mentioned above is not obtained through ownership of a piece of property but by personally fulfilling a certain functional role. If an organization is thought of as a molecule made of certain atoms, then the two different organizations have quite different atoms. For the capitalist corporation and the condominium, the atoms are the property shares (which are owned by people), while for a democratic organization (like the three considered above), the atoms are the people themselves.

We will therefore say that an organization is *people-based* if the membership rights are personal rights (i.e. the atomic building blocks are the people themselves), and that an organization is *property-based* if the membership rights are attached to property shares owned by people.

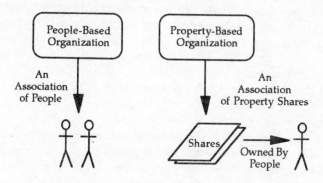

Figure 2.3 Two Basic Different Types of Organizations

This useful distinction shows up in ordinary language. In a democracy, the people vote, whereas in a corporation the shares vote, and in a condominium the units vote. In either case, it is people who ultimately cast votes but a citizen casts his or her vote while shareholders cast the votes on their shares and unit-owners cast the votes assigned to their units. The distinction also ties in with the inheritability test. In an association of persons, the death of the person forfeits that membership, but in an association of property shares, the property survives. Thus when a person dies, the heirs do not inherit the person's political vote but they would inherit any corporate stock or condominium units owned by the deceased.

There is another important aspect of the distinction, the allocation of voting rights. In a people-based organization (e.g. the three considered above), the voting rule is one-person/one-vote whereas in the property-based organization, the property owners will have differing numbers of votes depending on the number of their property shares (and the number of attached votes).

It might be helpful to review why there is equal voting in an association of *persons* (and not in an association of property). It is *not* because the people are assumed to have equal intelligence, equal skills, equal economic stake, or equal contribution to the organization. The reason is that—as persons—they are ends-in-themselves (in the Kantian phrase, see Ellerman, 1988c). Ends-in-themselves are incommensurate so there can be no common measure to weigh one more than the other; they must be treated equally. In contrast, property is commensurate (e.g. using market value as the measuring rod) so the share owners vote according to the different economic stakes in a property-based organization.

In the American employee ownership movement, the one-person/one-vote principle has become a symbol, if not a defining characteristic, of the democratic wing of the movement. It is the most prominent feature of the democratic firm as opposed to the worker-capitalist firm. But it is only the tip of the iceberg, the most visible part of the deep-lying differences between:

— the *democratic firm*—a people-based corporation based on implementing the democratic right of self-governance by assigning it as a personal right to the functional role of being managed in the firm, as opposed to

— the *worker-capitalist firm*—a property-based corporation where the workers alienate their governance rights to the corporation in the employment contract and where most of the same workers as property-owners own part or all the shares in the corporation.

This contrast between the democratic worker-owned firm and the worker-capitalist firm will be developed in more detail in the following chapter.

Democracy Denied by the Employment Contract, not Private Property

The Employment Contract

We saw in the previous chapter that capitalist production, i.e. production based on the employment contract denies workers the right to the (positive and negative) fruits of their labor. Yet people's right to the fruits of their labor has always been the natural basis for private property appropriation. Thus capitalist production, far from being founded on private property, in fact denies the natural basis for private property appropriation. In contrast, the system of economic democracy based on democratic worker-owned firms restores people's right to the fruits of their labor. Thus democratic firms, far from violating private property, restore the just basis for private property appropriation.

Thus to switch from capitalist firms to democratic firms is a way to transform and perfect the private property system by restoring the labor basis of appropriation. It is not private property that needs to be abolished—but the employment contract. In the switch-over from capitalist firms to democratic firms, the employment relation would be replaced with the membership relation.

A similar picture emerges when the firm is analyzed from the viewpoint of governance rather than property appropriation; the employment contract is the culprit, not private property. The employment contract is the rental relation applied to persons. It is now illegal to sell oneself; workers rent or hire themselves out.

> Since slavery was abolished, human earning power is forbidden by law to be capitalized. A man is not even free to sell himself: he must *rent* himself at a wage. (Samuelson, 1976, p. 52 [his italics])

When an entity, a person or a thing, is rented out, then a certain portion of the entity's services are sold. When a car is rented out for a day, a car-day of services are sold. When an apartment is rented out for a month, an apartment-month of services are sold. When a man is rented out for eight hours, eight man-hours of services are sold. The party renting the entity has the ownership of those services which gives that party the direct control rights over the use of the rented entity within the limits of the contract. Thus tenants are free to make their own decisions about using a rented apartment—but only within the constraints set by the rental contract.

It is the same when people are rented. The buyer of the services, the renter of the workers, is the employer. The employer has the direct control rights over the use of those services within the scope of the employment contract. The archaic name for the employer–employee relation is the "master–servant relation" (language still used in Agency Law). That authority relation is not now and never was a democratic relationship. The employer is not the representative of the employees; the employer does not act in the name of the employees. The right to govern the employees is transferred or alienated to the employer who then acts in his own name; it is not a delegation of authority.

There is the contrasting democratic authority relationship wherein authority is delegated to those who govern from the governed. Those who govern do so in the name of and on behalf of those who are governed. This is the relationship between the managers or governors in a democratic organization (political or economic) and those who are managed or governed.

Democratic and Undemocratic Constitutions

Both authority relations are based on "the consent of the governed." There are two diametrically opposite types of voluntary contracts or constitutions that can form the basis of constitutional governance:

— the Hobbesian constitution or *pactum subjectionis* wherein the rights of governance are alienated and transferred to the ruler, or
— the democratic constitution wherein the inalienable rights of governance are merely delegated or entrusted to the governors to use on behalf of the governed.

The distinction between these two opposite consent-based authority relations is basic to democratic theory. Sophisticated liberal defenders of undemocratic governments from the Middle Ages onward have argued that government was based on an implicit or explicit social contract of subjugation which transferred the right of governance to the ruler (see Ellerman, 1986a for that intellectual history). Early proponents of democracy tried to reinterpret the mandate of the ruler as a delegation rather than a transfer.

> This dispute also reaches far back into the Middle Ages. It first took a strictly juristic form in the dispute ... as to the legal nature of the ancient "translatio imperii" from the Roman people to the Princeps. One school explained this as a definitive and irrevocable alienation of power, the other as a mere concession of its use and exercise. ... On the one hand from the people's abdication the most absolute sovereignty of the prince might be deduced, ... On the other hand the assumption of a mere "concessio imperii" led to the doctrine of popular sovereignty. (Gierke, 1966, pp. 93–4)

"Translatio" or "concessio," transfer or delegation; that is the question.

That question is still with us. As noted previously, the employer is not the delegate or representative of the employees. The employment contract is a *transfer* of the management rights, not a delegation. Thus the employment contract is a limited workplace version of the Hobbesian constitution. The democratic firm is based on the opposite type of constitution, the democratic constitution. The board of directors is the parliament elected by those who are governed. The board selects the top manager (like the prime minister) who in turn assembles the management team. Management governs in the name of and on behalf of the governed.

Are Democracy and Private Property in Conflict?

Economic democracy requires the abolition of the employment relation, not the abolition of private property. But doesn't it

61

require the abolition of the conventional property-based corporation? Isn't that type of corporation undemocratic? Here we must be very careful; the analysis must be much more fine-grained than the crude Marxist slogans about the "private ownership of the means of production."

The capitalist corporation combines two different functions that must be peeled apart:

(1) the corporation as a holding company for owning certain assets and liabilities, and
(2) the corporation as the residual claimant in a production process.

A number of people can pool their assets together and clothe them in a corporate shell by setting up a corporation and putting in their capital assets as equity. That only creates a company in the first sense above. The company is only a holding company for these assets; the company is as yet "uninhabited." If the corporate assets were just leased out to other parties, that transaction could be handled by the shareholders or their attorneys all without anyone working in the company. The company would remain an asset-holding shell. There is no governance of people, only the administration of things. There is private property, but no employment contract.

It is only when the company wants to undertake some productive activity to produce a product or deliver a service that it would need to hire in employees, buy other inputs, undertake the productive operation, and then sell the resulting product or service. Then the company would be the residual claimant for that operation, bearing the costs and receiving the revenues. It is only in that second role that the corporation becomes an organization for the governance or management of people, the corporate employees. And it acquires that role precisely because of the employment contract. The employment contract is the Archimedean point that moves the capitalist world. From the conceptual viewpoint, the *capitalist* corporation is a "wholly owned subsidiary" of the employment contract.

We have differentiated the roles of private property and the employment contract in the capitalist corporation.

Without the employment contract, the corporation as an asset-holding shell is comparable to a condominium. The tenants in a condominium unit (whether a unit-owner or a renter) are not under the authority of the condominium association. The tenant has the direct control rights over the use of the apartment-unit within the constraints specified by the condominium rules (and the rental contract if the apartment is rented out).

In a similar fashion, an uninhabited asset-owning company might lease its assets out to other parties. The company would not have an authority relation (i.e. direct control rights) over the lessees. The lessees could use the leased assets within the constraints of the lease contract.

Is a capitalist corporation undemocratic? In which role? In its role as a depopulated asset-holding shell, it does not have an authority relation over any people at all. It would not then be an organization for the governing of people, only for the management of property. It thus would be neither democratic nor undemocratic since no people were governed. When a farmer manages his farmland property, we do not ask if he does so democratically or undemocratically since the management of his property does not involve an authority relationship over other people. In the same fashion, we may say that a conventional corporation that is without any employment contract and that operates solely as an asset-holding shell is neither democratic nor undemocratic. Yet it is a privately owned property-based organization. Thus there is no inherent conflict between "the private ownership of the means of production" and democratic rights in the workplace.

A conventional corporation only takes on an authority relation over people when it hires them as employees (managers or blue-collar workers). And, as we have seen, there *is* a conflict between democratic rights and the employment contract. Thus democratic rights require not the abolition of the private ownership of the means of production but of the employment contract. They require that conventional corporations not be abolished but only "depopulated" as a result of the abolition of the employment relation. To be employed productively, the assets would have to be leased to a democratic firm.

The reversal of the contract between capital and labor (so that labor hires capital) could also take place by internally restructuring a capitalist corporation as a democratic firm with the old shareholders' securities being restructured as participating debt securities.

Democracy can be married with private property in the workplace; the result of the union is the democratic worker-owned firm.

The *De Facto* Theory of Inalienable Rights

The analysis of capitalist production based on the labor theory of property (see previous chapter) culminated in an argument that the employment contract was a juridically invalid contract. It pretends to alienate that which is *de facto* inalienable, namely a person's *de facto* responsibility for the positive and negative results of his or her actions. This *de facto* inalienability of responsibility was illustrated using the example of the employee who commits a crime at the command of the employer. Then the legal authorities intervene, set aside the employment contract, and recognize the fact that the employee and employer cooperated together to commit the crime. They are jointly *de facto* responsible for it, and the law accordingly holds them legally responsible for it.

When the joint venture being carried out by employer and employees is not criminal, the employees do not suddenly become *de facto* instruments. However, the law then does not intervene. It accepts the employees' same *de facto* responsible cooperation with the employer as "fulfilling" the contract. The employer then has the legal role of having borne the costs of all the used-up inputs including the labor costs, so the employer has the undivided legal claim on the produced outputs. Thus the employer legally appropriates the whole product (i.e. the input-liabilities and the output-assets).

The critique does not assert that the employment contract is involuntary or socially coercive. The critique asserts that what the employees do voluntarily (i.e. voluntarily co-operate with the employer) does not fulfill the employment contract. Labor, in the sense of responsible human action, is *de facto* non-transferable, so the contract to buy and sell labor services is inherently invalid. The rights to the positive and negative fruits of one's labor are thus inalienable rights.

This argument is not new; it was originally developed by radical abolitionists as a critique of the voluntary self-sale contract and it was the basis for the antislavery doctrine of inalienable rights developed during the Enlightenment (see Ellerman, 1986a). The employment contract is the self-rental contract, the contract to sell a limited portion of one's labor—as opposed to selling all of one's labor, "rump and stump" (Marx, 1906, p. 186) as in the self-sale contract. But *de facto* responsibility does not suddenly become factually transferable when it is "sold" by the hour or day rather than by the lifetime. Thus economic democrats are the modern abolitionists who apply the same inalienable rights critique to the employment contract that their predecessors applied to the self-sale contract.

This *de facto* theory of inalienable rights was also developed as a part of democratic theory. There it was directed not against the individual self-enslavement contract but against the collective version of the contract, the Hobbesian *pactum subjectionis*. In questions of governance (as opposed to production), the emphasis is on decision-making (as opposed to responsibility). But the basic facts are the same. Decision-making capacity is *de facto* inalienable. A person cannot in fact alienate his or her decision-making capacity just as he or she cannot alienate *de facto* responsibility. "Deciding to do as one is told" is only another way of deciding what to do.

Here again it is useful to contrast what one can do with oneself with what one can do with a thing such as a widget-making machine. When the machine is leased out to another individual, the machine can in fact be turned over to be employed by that "employer." The employer can then use the machine without any personal involvement of the machine-owner. The employer is solely *de facto* responsible for the results of said use. Furthermore, the employer has the direct control rights over the use of the machine. The employer decides to use the machine to do X rather then Y (within the scope of the lease contract), and the machine-owner is not involved in that decision making. Thus decision-making about the particular use of the machine and the responsibility for the results of the machine's services are *de facto* alienable from the machine-owner to the machine-employer.

The employment contract applies the same legal super-structure to the very different case when the worker takes the place of the machine. Then the decision-making and the responsibility for the results of the services is not *de facto* transferable from the worker to the employer.

People cannot in fact alienate or transfer decision-making capability—but persons can delegate the authority to make a decision to other persons acting as their representatives or agents. The first persons, the principals, then accept and ratify the decisions indicated by their delegates, representatives, or agents.

The Hobbesian *pactum subjectionis* is the political consti-tution wherein a people legally alienate and transfer their decision-making rights over their own affairs to a Sovereign (see Philmore, 1982 for an intellectual history of the *liberal* contractarian defense of slavery and autocracy). Since human decision-making capability is *de facto* inalienable, Enlighten-ment democratic theory argued that the Hobbesian contract was inherently invalid.

There is, at least, *one* right that cannot be ceded or abandoned: the right to personality. Arguing upon this principle the most influential writers on politics in the seventeenth century rejected the conclusions drawn by Hobbes. They charged the great logician with a contra-diction in terms. If a man could give up his personality he would cease being a moral being... This fundamental right, the right to personality, includes in a sense all the others. To maintain and to develop his personality is a universal right. It ... cannot, therefore, be transferred from one individual to another... There is no *pactum sub-jectionis*, no act of submission by which man can give up the state of a free agent and enslave himself. (Cassirer, 1963, p. 175)

The employment contract can be viewed both as a limited individual version of the rump-and-stump labor contract (the self-sale contract) and as a limited economic version of the

Hobbesian collective contract. The employees legally alienate and transfer to the employer their decision-making rights over the use of their labor within the scope of their employment. Thus the other branch of inalienable rights theory, the critique of the Hobbesian contract, can also be applied against the employment contract.

The critique of the employment contract based on the *de facto* inalienability of responsibility and decision-making thus descends to modern times from the abolitionism and democratic theory of the Enlightenment which applied the critique to the self-sale contract and the *pactum subjectionis*.

3

The Democratic Firm

Theoretical Basis for the Democratic Firm

The Democratic Principle and the Labor Theory

We now start the descent from first principles—the labor theory of property and democratic theory—down to the structure of the democratic worker-owned company.

In the world today, the main form of enterprise in capitalist and socialist countries is based on renting human beings (privately or publicly). Our task is to construct the alternative. In the alternative type of firm, employment by the firm is replaced with membership in the firm. How can the corporation be taken apart and reconstructed without the employment relation? How can the labor principle at the basis of private property appropriation be built into corporate structure? How can the democratic principle of self-governance be built into corporate structure?

In a capitalist corporation, the shareholders own, as property rights, the conventional ownership bundle of rights.

❶ The voting rights (e.g., to elect the Board of Directors),

❷ The rights to the residual or net income, and

❸ The rights to the net value of the current corporate assets and liabilities.

Residual Claimant Rights = Membership Rights

Figure 3.1   The Conventional Ownership Bundle

Restructuring the corporation to create a democratic firm does not mean just finding a new set of owners (such as the

68

"employees") for that bundle of rights. It means taking the bundle apart and restructuring the rights so that the whole nature of "corporate ownership" is changed.

The democratic firm is based on two fundamental principles:

Democratic principle of self-government: people's inalienable right to self-govern all of their human activities (political or economic), and

Labor theory of property: people's inalienable right to appropriate the (positive and negative) fruits of their labor.

These two principles are correlated respectively with the first two rights in the conventional ownership bundle:

— the voting rights and
— the residual or net income rights

which are attached to the pure (current) residual claimant's role and which will be called the *membership rights*. We will see that:

the democratic principle implies that the voting rights should be assigned to the workers, and
the labor theory of property implies that the residual rights should be assigned to the workers.

Implementing the Democratic Principle in an Organization

How are the two fundamental principles realized in the design of organizations?

> The principle of democratic self-government or self-management is built into the structure of an institution by assigning the right to elect the governors to the functional role of being governed.

The only people who are under the authority of the management (i.e. who take orders from the managers) of an economic enterprise are the people who work in the enterprise. Therefore the democratic principle is implemented in a firm by assigning to the people who work in the firm the voting rights to elect those managers (or to elect the board that selects the managers).

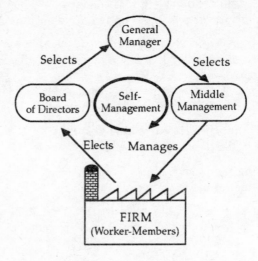

Figure 3.2   Governance of Democratic Firm

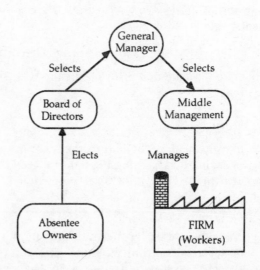

Figure 3.3   Governance of Non-Democratic Firm

In contrast, the ultimate control rights in a non-democratic firm are not held by those who are governed.

Note that the democratic principle assigns the right to elect those who govern to those who are *governed*. There are a number of outside groups whose rightful interests (i.e. property or personal interests protected by rights) are only *affected* by company activities such as the consumers, shareholders, suppliers, and the local residents. By what we called the "affected interests principle," those outside interests should be protected by a voluntary interface between the enterprise and the affected parties. By the market relationship (where more choice between firms is preferred to less), customers and suppliers can largely protect their interests. For externalities such as pollution, governments can establish emission restrictions, pollution taxes, or subsidies for pollution control equipment.

The democratic principle assigns the direct control right giving the ultimate authority for governance decisions to the governed. Since the external parties do not fall under the authority of the management of the firm (that is, do not take orders from the managers), the democratic principle does not assign the external parties a direct control right to elect that management.

In summary,

Affected Interests Principle: the veto to those only affected,
Democratic Principle: the vote to those who are governed.

Implementing the Labor Theory in an Organization

The *"labor theory"* has always had two quite different interpretations:

(A) as a *theory of value* holding that price or value is determined by labor, and

(B) as a *theory of property* holding that workers should get the fruits (both positive and negative) of their labor.

Neo-classical economics has focused on the labor theory of value as a theory of price, but it is "the labor theory" as a theory of property, that is, the *labor theory of property*, that determines the structure of property rights in a democratic firm.

71

The positive fruits of the labor of the people working in an enterprise (workers including managers) are the new assets produced as outputs which could be represented as Q. The negative fruits of their labor are the liabilities for the inputs used up in the production process. The used-up inputs could be represented by K (all non-labor inputs such as capital services and the services of land).

The firm as a corporate entity legally owns those assets Q and holds those liabilities for the used-up K. Therefore the people who work in a firm will jointly appropriate the positive and negative fruits of their joint labor when *they* are the legal members of the firm.

> The labor theory of property is implemented in the legal structure of a company by assigning the residual rights to the functional role of working in the company.

If p is the unit price of the outputs Q and R is the unit rental rate for the input services K, then the residual pQ–RK is the revenue minus the non-labor costs. In a democratic firm, that residual would be the labor income accruing to the workers as wages and salaries paid out during the year and as surplus or profits determined at the end of the fiscal year. Thus both "wages" and "profits" are labor income; there is only a timing difference between them.

The Democratic Labor-based Firm

Definition of the Legal Structure

In a capitalist corporation, the membership rights (voting and profit rights) are part of the property rights attached to the shares which are transferable on the stock market or in private transactions. In a democratic firm, the membership rights are not property rights at all; they are personal rights assigned to the functional role of working in the firm, i.e. assigned to the workers as workers (not as capital suppliers).

In particular, the democratic principle states that the right to elect those who govern or manage (for example, the municipal government) should be assigned to the functional role of being governed or managed (e.g. living in the municipality). Hence the democratic principle assigns the voting rights to elect the board of directors to the workers as their personal rights (because they have the functional role of being managed). After an initial probationary period, it is "up or out"; a worker is either accepted into membership or let go so that all long-term workers in the firm are members. Upon retiring or otherwise leaving the firm, the member gives up the membership rights so that the votes always go to those being governed.

In a similar manner, the labor theory of property states that the rights to the produced outputs (Q) and the liabilities for the used-up inputs (K) should be assigned to the functional role of producing those outputs and liabilities. Hence the labor theory assigns the residual rights to the workers as their personal rights (because they have the functional role of producing those outputs and using up those inputs). If a worker left enterprise A and joined firm B, then he or she would forfeit any share in the future residual of A (since he or she ceased to produce that residual) and would gain a residual share in firm B.

The democratic principle and the labor theory of property are thus legally institutionalized in a corporation by assigning the two membership rights, the voting rights and the residual claimant rights, to the functional role of working in the firm. When membership rights are thus assigned to the role of labor, then the rights are said to be *labor-based*. When membership rights are owned as property or capital, the membership rights are to be *capital-based* or *capital-ist* even when those rights are owned by the employees. In the democratic labor-based firm, the workers are the masters of their enterprise—and they are the masters *as workers*, not as "small capital-ists."

The third set of rights in the conventional ownership bundle, the rights to the net value of the current assets and liabilities, are quite different. They represent the value of the original endowment plus the value of the past fruits of the labor of the firm's current and past members reinvested in the firm. The

73

rights due to the members' past labor should be respected as property rights eventually recoupable by the current and past members.

The job of restructuring the conventional ownership bundle to create the legal structure of a *democratic firm* (also "democratic labor-based firm" or "democratic worker-owned firm") can now be precisely specified.

❶ The voting rights.

❷ The rights to the net income.

} Membership Rights Assigned as Personal Rights to Worker's Role.

❸ The rights to the net value of the current corporate assets and liabilities.

} Property Rights Recorded in Internal Capital Accounts.

Figure 3.4 Restructured Ownership Bundle in a Democratic Firm

The first two rights, the voting and residual rights, i.e. the membership rights, should be assigned as personal rights to the functional role of working in the firm. The third right to the value of the net assets should remain a property right recoupable in part by the current and past members who invested and reinvested their property to build up those net assets.

The Social Aspects of Democratic Labor-based Firms

The democratic labor-based firm does not just supply a new set of owners for the conventional ownership bundle of rights. It completely changes the nature of the rights and thus the nature of the corporation.

Who "owns" a democratic labor-based firm? The question is not well-posed—like the question of who "owns" a freedman. The conventional ownership bundle has been cut apart and restructured in a democratic firm. The membership rights were completely transformed from property or ownership rights into personal rights held by the workers. Thus the workers do hold the "ownership rights" but not *as ownership rights*; those membership rights are held *as personal rights*. Thus it may be more appropriate to call the workers in a democratic firm "members" rather than "owners." Nevertheless, they are the

74

"owners" in the sense they do hold the "ownership rights" (as personal rights), and it is in that sense that we can call a democratic labor-based firm a "worker-owned firm."

The change in the nature of the membership rights from property rights to personal rights implies a corresponding change in the nature of the corporation itself. No longer is it "owned" by anyone. The "ownership" or membership rights are indeed held by the current workers (so they will self-manage their work and reap the full fruits of their labor) but they do not own these rights as their property which they need to buy or can sell. The workers qualify for the membership rights by working in the firm (beyond a certain probationary period) and they forfeit those rights upon leaving.

Since those membership rights are not property which could be bought or sold, the democratic labor-based corporation is not a piece of property. It is a *democratic social institution.*

It is useful to contrast the democratic labor-based corporation with a democratic city, town, or community. It is sometimes thought that, say, a municipal government is "social" because it represents "everyone" while a particular set of workers in an enterprise is "private" because that grouping is not all-inclusive. But no grouping is really "all-inclusive"; each city excludes the neighboring cities, each province excludes the other provinces, and each country excludes the other countries. Only "humanity" is all-inclusive—yet no government represents all of humanity.

Governments are "all-inclusive" in that they represent everyone who legally resides in a certain *geographical* area, the jurisdiction of the local, state, or national government. But the management of a democratic firm is *also* "all-inclusive" in that it represents everyone who works in the enterprise. It is a community of those who *work* together, just as a city or town is a community of those who *live* together in a certain area. Why shouldn't a grouping of people together by common labor be just as "social" as the grouping of people together by a common area of residence?

The genuinely "social" aspect of a democratically governed community is that the community itself is not a piece of property. The right to elect those who govern the community is a personal right attached to the functional role of being governed, that is, to legally residing within the jurisdiction of that government. Citizens cannot buy those rights and may not sell those rights—they are personal rights rather than property rights.

In contrast, consider a town, village, or protective association (see Nozick, 1974) that was "owned" by a prince or warlord as his property, a property that could be bought and sold. That would be a "government" of a sort, but it would not be a *res publica*; that "government" would not be a social or public institution.

The democratic corporation is a social community, a community of work rather than a community of residence. It is a republic or *res publica* of the workplace. The ultimate governance rights are assigned as personal rights to those who are governed by the management, that is, to the people who work in the firm. And in accordance with the property rights version of the "labor theory of value," the rights to the residual claimant's role are assigned as personal rights to the people who produce the outputs by using up the inputs of the firm, that is, to the workers of the firm. This analysis shows how a firm can be socialized and yet remain "private" in the sense of not being government-owned.

Capital Rights in Democratic Firms

What About the Net Asset Value of a Corporation?

We have so far focused most of our attention on the membership rights (the first two rights in the ownership bundle) in our treatment of the democratic firm. Now we turn to the third right, the right to the net asset value. That is the hard one. The major difference between cooperatives (e.g. traditional stock cooperatives, common-ownership co-ops, or Mondragon-type cooperatives) is in how they treat that third right. One of the most important and most difficult aspects of enterprise reform in the socialist countries is again in the treatment of those property rights.

The value of that third right is the net asset value, the value of the assets (depreciated by use but perhaps with adjustments for inflation) minus the value of the enterprise's liabilities. The net asset value may or may not be approximated by the net *book* value depending on the bookkeeping procedures in use (see Ellerman, 1982 for a treatment of such accounting questions). Of more importance, the net asset value is not the same as the so-called "value of a [capitalist] corporation" even if all the assets have their true market values. The "value of a corporation" is the net asset value *plus* the net value of the fruits of all the future workers in the enterprise. In a democratic firm, the net value of the fruits of the future workers' labor should accrue to those future workers, not the present workers. Hence our discussion of the capital rights of the current workers quite purposely focuses on the net asset value, not the "value of the corporation."

The net asset value arises from the original endowment or paid-in capital of the enterprise plus (minus) the retained profits (losses) from each year's operations. Thus it is not necessarily even the fruits of the labor of the current workers; the endowment may have come from other parties and the *past* workers who made the past profits and losses. Hence the third right, the right to the net asset value, should *not* be treated as a personal right attached to the functional role of working in the firm.

There is considerable controversy about how the net asset value should be treated. One widespread socialist belief is that the net asset value must be collectively owned as in the English common-ownership firms or the Yugoslav self-managed firms; otherwise there would be "private ownership of the means of production." To analyze this view, it must first be recalled that the control (voting) and profit rights have been partitioned away from the rights to the net asset value. The phrase "private ownership of the means of production" usually does include specifically the rights to control and reap the profits from the means of production. But those rights have been restructured as personal rights assigned to labor in the democratic firm. Hence the remaining right to the net asset value does *not* include the control and profit rights traditionally associated with "equity capital" or with the "ownership of the means of production."

Let us suppose that it is still argued that any private claim (for example, by past workers) on the net asset value of a democratic firm would be "appropriating social capital to private uses." This argument has much merit for that portion of the net asset value that comes from some original social endowment. But what about that portion of the net asset value that comes from retained earnings in the past?

In a democratic firm, the past workers could, in theory, have used their control and profit rights to pay out all the net earnings instead of retaining any in the firm. Suppose they retained some earnings to finance a machine. Why should those workers lose their claim on that value—except as they use up the machine? Why should the fruits of their labor suddenly become "social property" simply because they choose to reinvest it in their company?

Consider the following thought-experiment. Instead of retaining the earnings to finance a machine, suppose the workers paid out the earnings as bonuses, deposited them all in one savings bank, and then took out a loan from the bank to finance the machine using the deposits as collateral.

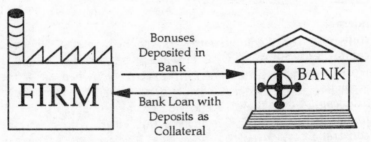

Figure 3.5   Indirect Self-Finance through a Bank

Then the workers would not lose the value of those earnings since that value is represented in the balance in their savings accounts in the bank. And the enterprise still gets to finance the machine. Since the finance was raised by a loan, there was no private claim on the social equity capital of the enterprise and thus no violation of "socialist principles." The loan capital is capital hired by labor; it gets only interest with no votes and no share of the profits.

Now we come to the point of the thought-experiment. How is it different in principle if we simply leave the bank out and move the workers' savings accounts into the firm itself? Instead of going through the whole circuitous loop of paying out the earnings, depositing them in the bank's savings accounts, and then borrowing the money back—suppose the firm directly retains the earnings, credits the workers' savings accounts in the firm, and buys the machine. The capital balance represented in the savings accounts is essentially *loan* capital. It is hired by labor, it receives interest, and it has no votes or profit shares. Such accounts have been developed in the Mondragon worker cooperatives, and they are called *internal capital accounts.*

One lesson of this thought-experiment is that once the control and profit rights have been separated off from the net asset value, any remaining claim on that value is essentially a debt claim receiving interest but no votes or profits. "Equity capital" (in the traditional sense) *does not exist* in the democratic firm; *labor* has taken on the residual claimant's role.

Capital Accounts as Flexible Internal Debt Capital

Internal capital accounts for the worker-members in a democratic corporation are a form of debt capital. Labor is hiring capital, and some of the hired capital is provided by the workers themselves and is recorded in the internal capital accounts. These internal capital accounts represent *internal debt capital* owed to members, as opposed to *external* debt owed to outsiders. Instead of debt and equity as in a conventional corporation, a democratic firm with internal capital accounts has external and internal debt.

How does internal debt differ from external debt, and how does an internal capital account differ from a savings account? Any organization, to survive, must have a way to meet its deficits. There seem to be two widely used methods: (1) tax, and (2) lien. Governments use the power to tax citizens, and unions similarly use the power to assess or tax members to cover their deficits. Other organizations place a lien on certain assets so that deficits can be taken out of the value of those assets. For instance, it is a common practice to require damage deposits from people renting apartments. Damages are assessed against the deposit before the remainder is returned to a departing tenant.

A free-standing democratic firm must similarly find a way to ultimately cover its deficits. Assuming members could always quit and could not then be assessed for possible losses accumulating in the current year, the more likely method is to place a lien against any money owed to the member by the firm. Each member's share of the losses incurred while the worker was a member of the firm would be subtracted from the firm's internal debt or internal capital account balance for the member. This procedure would be agreed to in the constitution or ground rules of the democratic firm. Losses, of course, may not be subtracted from the external debts owed to outsiders. Hence internal debt in a democratic firm would have the unique characteristic of being downwardly flexible or "soft" in comparison with external "hard" debt. It is thus also different from a savings account in a bank which would not be debited for a part of the bank's losses.

In the comparison between a democratic firm and a democratic political government, the firm's liabilities are analogous to the country's national debt. The internal capital accounts, as internal debt capital, are analogous to the domestic portion of the national debt owed to the country's own citizens. The differences arise because of the two different methods of covering deficits. The firm uses the lien method while political governments rely on the power to tax.

The firm's lien against a member's internal capital account also motivates the common practice of requiring a fixed initial membership fee to be paid in from payroll or out of pocket. Then there is an initial balance in each member's account to cover a member's share of losses during his or her first year of work.

Profits or year-end surpluses, like losses or year-end deficits, would be allocated among the members in accordance with their labor, not their capital, since labor is hiring capital and is thus the residual claimant. The labor of each member is commonly measured by their wage or salary, or, in some cases, by the hours regardless of the pay rate. In worker cooperatives, that measure of each member's labor is called "patronage" and net earnings are allocated in accordance with labor patronage. When the net earnings are negative, the losses are allocated between the capital accounts in accordance with labor. Thus the system of internal capital accounts provides a risk-absorbing mechanism with a labor-based allocation of losses.

The Internal Capital Accounts Rollover

"Allocation" is not the same thing as cash distribution. There are good practical arguments for *not* paying out current profits as current labor dividends. The immediate payout of current profits promotes a "hand-to-mouth" mentality and fails to tie the workers' interests to the long term interests of the enterprise. By retaining the profits and crediting that value to the capital accounts, the workers need to insure that the enterprise prospers so their value can eventually be recovered.

When should the accounts be paid out? One idea is to leave the account until the worker retires or otherwise terminates work in the enterprise, and then to pay out the account over a period of years. There are several reasons why that termination payout scheme is not a good idea.

By waiting until termination or retirement for the account payout, the accounts of the older workers would be much larger than those of the younger workers and thus the older workers would be bearing a grossly unequal portion of the risk. Risk-bearing should be more equally shared between the older and younger workers. Moreover, it would create an incentive for the older and better trained workers to quit in order to cash out their account and reduce their risks. For young workers, retirement is too distant a time horizon. Current profits would be an almost meaningless incentive for them if the profits could not be recovered until retirement. And finally cash flow planning would be difficult if the cash demands of account payouts were a function of unpredictable terminations.

These problems with the termination payout scheme are alleviated by an "account rollover scheme" wherein the account entries are paid out after a fixed time period. The allocations to the accounts are dated. Cash payouts should be used to reduce the older entries in the capital accounts. If an account entry has survived the risk of being debited to cover losses for, say, five years, then the entry should be paid out. That is sometimes called a "rollover" (as in rolling over or turning over an inventory) and it tends to equalize the balances in the capital accounts and thus equalize the risks borne by the different members.

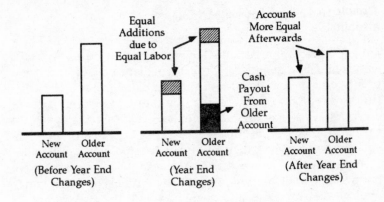

Figure 3.6   Internal Capital Account Rollover

Current retained labor patronage allocation adds to all members' accounts (equal additions assumed in the above illustration), and then the cash payouts reduce the balance in the larger and older accounts—thereby tending to equalize all the accounts. The incentive to terminate is relieved since the account entries are paid out after the fixed time period whether the member terminates or not. And cash flow planning is eased since the firm knows the payout requirements, say, five years ahead of time.

Instead of receiving wages and current profit dividends, workers would receive wages and the five-year-lagged rollover payments. New workers would not receive the rollover payments during their first five years. They would be, as it were, paying off the "mortgage" held by the older workers—without being senior enough to start receiving the "mortgage payments" themselves.

A Collective Internal Capital Account

In a socialist country, some of a democratic firm's net asset value might be endowed from a governmental unit, and there is no reason why that value should ultimately accrue to the workers of the enterprise. Hence there should be a *collective account* to contain the value of the collective endowment not attributable to the members.

Assets	Liabilities
Cash	External Debts
Inventory	Individual Capital Accounts
Equipment	(Internal Debts)
Plant	Collective Account

Figure 3.7 Balance Sheet with Internal Capital Accounts

The net asset value (defined as the value of the assets minus the value of the external debts) equals the sum of the balances in the individual capital accounts and the collective account. Two other accounts, a temporary collective account called a "suspense account" and a "loan balance account," will be introduced in the later model of a hybrid democratic firm in order to accommodate ESOP-type transactions.

There is another reason for a collective account, namely, self-insurance against the risks involved in paying out the members' capital accounts. After retirement, the enterprise must pay out to a member the remaining balance in the worker's capital account. In an uncertain world, it would be foolish to think that an enterprise could always eventually pay out 100 per cent of its retained earnings. Any scheme to finance that payout would have to pay the price of bearing the risk of default. One option is always self-insurance. Instead of promising to ultimately pay back 100 per cent of retained earnings to the members, the firm should only promise, say, a 70 per cent or a 50 per cent payback. That is, 30 per cent to 50 per cent of the retained earnings could always be credited as a "self-insurance allocation" to the collective account, and that would serve to insure

83

that the other 70 per cent to 50 per cent could ultimately be paid back to the members.

The self-insurance allocation should also be applied to losses. That is, when retained earnings are negative, 30 per cent to 50 per cent should be debited to the collective account with the remaining losses distributed among the members' individual capital accounts in accordance with labor patronage. Thus the self-insurance allocation would dampen both the up-swings and down-swings in net income.

The current members of a democratic firm with a large collective account should not be allowed to appropriate the collective account by voluntary dissolution (after paying out their individual accounts). Any net value left after liquidating the assets and paying out the external and internal debts should accrue to charitable organizations or to *all* past members.

Financing Internal Capital Account Payouts

In an economy where all firms were organized as democratic labor-based firms, there would be no equity capital markets since membership rights would not be property rights at all. However, there could and should be a vigorous market in debt capital instruments such as bonds, debentures, and even variable interest or "participating" debt securities.

How can democratic firms finance the payouts of their internal capital accounts? For a debt instrument with a finite maturity date, a company must eventually pay out the principal amount of the loan. However, a capitalist firm does not have to ever pay out the issued value of an equity share. A democratic firm could obtain the same effect by issuing perpetual debt instruments which pay interest but have no maturity date. Such a debt security is sometimes called a *consol* because they were once used by the British to consolidate their war debt (also called a *perpetuity* or a *perpetual annuity*, see Brealey and Myers, 1984). If the firm ever wants to pay off the principal value of a consol, it simply buys it back.

A democratic firm could use consols to pay out the rollover or the closing balance in an internal capital account. To increase the consol's resale value on debt markets, many firms could pool the risks by issuing the consols through a government, quasi-public, or cooperative financial institution or bank.

The pooling bank would pay a lower interest rate on the face value of the consol than the firms pay to it; the difference between the interest rates would cover the risks of default and the transactions costs. The allocation to the collective account for the purpose of self-insurance would not then be necessary since the cost of risk would be borne by the firm in the form of the interest differential. Since the consols would be guaranteed by the pooling institution (not the firm), workers could resell them without significant penalty.

The balance in a worker's internal capital account is a property right, not a personal right. For instance, if a worker-member dies, his or her vote and right to a residual share are extinguished but the right to the balance in the account passes to the heirs. Since the balance in the account is a property right, why can't the worker sell it? The only reason is the lien the enterprise has against the account to cover the worker's share of future losses (while the worker is a member). But if the balance is large enough (in spite of the rollover) or the worker is near enough to retirement, then part of the account *could* be paid out in salable consols (in addition to the rollover payouts). Internal capital accounts could also be paid out using *variable income* or "participating" securities.

Participating Securities

Since democratic organizations can only issue debt instruments, greater creativity should be applied to the design of new forms of corporate debt. Some risks could be shared with creditors by a reverse form of profit-sharing where the interest rate was geared to some objective measure of enterprise performance.

In a worker-owned firm, conventional preferred stock would not work well since it is geared to common stock. Ordinarily, common stockholders can only get value out of the corporation by declaring dividends on the common stock. Preferred stock has value because it is "piggy-backed" onto the common stock dividends. Dividends up to a certain percentage of face value must be paid on preferred stock before any common stock dividends can be paid. Preferred stockholders do not need control rights since they can assume the common stockholders will follow their own interests.

The preferred stockholders are like tax collectors that charge their tax on any value the common stockholders take out the front door. But that theory breaks down if the common stockholders have a *back door*—a way to extract value from the company without paying the tax to the preferred stockholders.

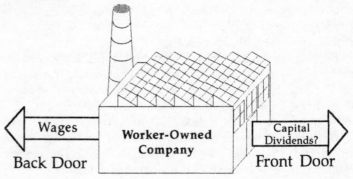

Figure 3.8 The Back Door Problem

That is the situation in a worker-owned company where the employees own the bulk of the common stock. They can always take their value out the "back door" of wages, bonuses, and benefits without paying the "tax" to the preferred stockholders. Hence the valuation mechanism for preferred stock breaks down in worker-owned companies. For similar reasons, absentee ownership of a minority of common stock would not make much sense in a worker-owned company; the workers would have little incentive to pay common dividends out the front door to absentee minority shareholders when the back door is open. *Discretionary* payments won't be made out the front door when the back door is open.

There are two ways to repair this problem in worker-owned companies:

— charge the preferred stock "tax" at all doors (front and back), or

— make the payout to preferred stockholders more mandatory and thus independent of what goes out the doors.

The first option leads to a form of non-voting preferred stock that would be workable for worker-owned companies where the preferred "dividend" is required and is geared to some other measure of the total value accruing to the worker-owners.

The second option pushes in the direction of a debt instrument—perhaps with a variable income feature. The interest could be variable but mandatory, geared to the company's "value-added" (revenue minus non-labor costs) to establish a form of profit-sharing in reverse (labor sharing profits with capital).

The two resulting conceptions are about the same: a non-voting preferred stock with a required "dividend" geared to some measure of the workers' total payout, and a perpetual bond with a variable return geared to value-added. Debt-equity hybrids are sometimes called "dequity." This general sort of non-voting, variable income, perpetual security could be called a *"participating dequity security"* since outside capital suppliers participate in the variability of the value-added. Jaroslav Vanek (1977, Chapter 11) describes a similar "variable income debenture" and Roger McCain (1977, pp. 358-9) likewise considers a "risk participation bond."

A debt instrument where interest is only payable if the company has a certain level of net income is called an "income bond" (see Brealey and Myers, 1984, p. 519). Dividends on preferred and common stock is paid at the discretion of the board of directors whereas the interest on an income bond *must* be paid if the company has a pre-specified level of accounting net income.

There is also a special type of income bond with two levels of interest; some interest is fixed, and then an additional interest or "dividend" is only payable if the company has sufficient income. These partly fixed-interest and partly variable-interest bonds are called "participating bonds" or "profit-sharing bonds" (Donaldson and Pfahl, 1963, p. 192). A participating consol would be a perpetual security with the participation feature.

Could large public markets be developed for such participating securities? Yes, such securities would closely approximate the dispersed equity shares in the large public stock markets in the United States and Europe. With the separation of ownership and control in the large quoted corporations, the vote is of little use to small shareholders. The notion that a publicly-quoted company can "miss a dividend" means that the dividend is sliding along the scale from being totally discretionary towards being more expected or required. Thus dispersed equity shares in large quoted corporations already function much like non-voting, variable income, perpetual securities, i.e. as participating dequity securities. Thus public markets in participating dequity securities not only can exist but in effect already do.

Mutual Funds for Participating Securities

It was previously noted that the market value of fixed-income securities would be enhanced if they were issued by a financial intermediary which could pool together the securities of a number of enterprises.

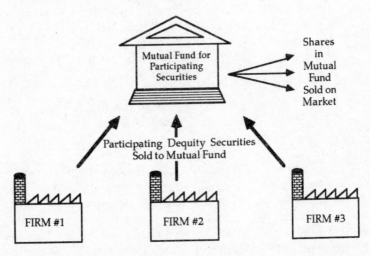

Figure 3.9 Pooling Participating Securities in a Mutual Fund

That application of the "insurance principle" would reduce the riskiness of the mixed-interest participating securities. There could be a "mutual fund" or "unit trust" that pools together the participating securities of enterprises it felt had good profit potential. Risk-taking individuals could buy securities directly from companies, while more risk-adverse individuals could buy shares of mutual funds that pooled together participating securities from many companies.

Workers receiving participating securities from their company could sell them directly for cash, hold them and receive interest, or swap them for shares in the mutual fund carrying that company's participating securities which could then be held or sold.

The participating securities also reduce risk for the company. The variable interest portion automatically reduces the interest charges when the company takes a downturn. The security-holder then gets less so the security-holder has shared the risk. The interest charges go up when the firm does well—but not beyond the maximum variable-interest cap. Thus the participating securities work to reduce the variance or variability of the net income for the company as a whole. Participating dequity securities allow democratic firms to utilize the risk allocative efficiency of public capital markets without putting the membership rights up for sale.

Aside from diversifying risk, the other major use of participating securities is to pay out the internal capital accounts of workers due to receive a "rollover" payment or who have retired or otherwise terminated work in the company. A public capital market in participating securities allows workers to capitalize the value of their internal capital accounts without the company itself having to "provide the market."

Do Democratic Firms Suffer a "Financial Disadvantage"?

Are democratic firms at a disadvantage since they cannot sell equity shares? Some perspective on this question can be gained if we consider the political analogue. Consider the imaginary world of *Nozickia* where the functions of government are taken over by "dominant protective associations" (Nozick, 1974, 113) organized as corporations with marketable shares. Then "governments" would be able to raise money by selling *equity* in addition to issuing more debt. There could be large developed markets in both debt and equity instruments issued by these governments. International financial institutions would be accustomed to both methods of financing governments.

Suppose that in this *completely privatized world* of marketable property rights, there arose the idea of a political democracy. Instead of being marketable property rights, the governance rights in a country were to be converted into personal rights or human rights attached to the functional role of residing in the country and being governed by that government. The government would then be social-ized; it would be a social institution rather than a piece of private property. Would such a government be possible? "Experts" would applaud the idealism of such a government but would doubt its financial feasibility. How could it compete for finance since it had cut itself off from all sources of external equity? Given the choice, large investors would often rather buy control rights when they invest in financial instruments. And, given the choice, political entrepreneurs founding new governments would rather package the governance rights as property rights that could eventually be capitalized—instead of as personal rights that could not be sold.

How could the idea of a political democracy have a chance? Yet, today political democracy is widely, if not universally, recognized as a political ideal. Like a democratic firm, a political democracy has no equity capital, only debt capital. All democracies, political or economic, have the financial disadvantage that the governance rights are not "for sale." Political democracies even have the same distinction between external debts owed to foreigners and internal debt capital (the domestic portion of the "National Debt") in the form of savings bonds and treasury notes held by citizens. Internal debt capital in a political democracy is, however, not flexible since deficits are covered ultimately by taxes or other means rather than by liens on citizens' internal debt capital.

Democratic governments "suffer" the same "financial disadvantage" as democratic firms of not being able to raise finance by selling equity shares. Yet, the fact is that governments are financed without selling equity. Similar transformations in financial institutions and markets would be necessary in an economic democracy. In an economy of democratic worker-managed firms, two markets would not exist. Like the market for equity shares in the government, the market for equity shares in firms (or for debt convertible into equity) would not exist. And like the market in political votes, the labor market would not exist (since labor would always be the residual claimant). There would be a job market in the sense of people looking for firms they could join, but it would not be a labor market in the sense of the selling of labor in the employment contract.

PART II
Worker Ownership in America and Europe

4

Worker Cooperatives

Introduction: Worker Ownership in America

In the second half of the nineteenth century, the first American trade unions of national scope, the National Trade Union and the Knights of Labor, saw their ultimate goal as a Cooperative Commonwealth where the wage system would be replaced by people working for themselves in worker cooperatives. Around the turn of the century, these reform unions were replaced by the business unions which accepted the wage system and sought to increase wages and benefits within that system through collective bargaining. During the Depression, there was an upsurge of self-help cooperatives, and after World War II there was a burst of worker cooperative development in the plywood industry of the Pacific Northwest. The plywood cooperatives used a traditional stock cooperative structure which mitigated against their long term survival as cooperatives.

In recent decades there have been two trends in American worker ownership, one minor and one major. The minor trend was the development of worker cooperatives that grew out of the civil rights and antiwar movements of the 1960s. The worker cooperative or collective was the form of business that suited the alternatives movement of the 1970s and 1980s. Many of the worker cooperatives looked more to the Mondragon cooperatives in the Basque country in Spain than to the American past for their inspiration. We will analyze the Mondragon-type worker cooperative in this chapter, not because it has been numerically important in the American economy, but because it represents a relatively pure form of democratic worker ownership.

The major trend in American worker ownership has been the development of the employee stock ownership plans or ESOPs.

95

The ESOP movement offers many lessons about worker ownership, both positive and negative. It is a very interesting case study in the rise of significant worker ownership in the midst of a capitalist economy. Of particular interest are the divergences between the public ideology of the ESOP movement and the reality of the ESOP structure. ESOPs are discussed in the next two chapters.

Worker Cooperatives in General

Existing worker-owned companies will be analyzed by considering the restructuring (or lack of it) for the conventional ownership bundle of rights: (1) the voting rights, (2) the profit or residual rights, and (3) the net asset rights.

All cooperatives have two broad characteristics:

(1) voting on a one-person/one-vote basis, and
(2) allocation of the net savings or residual to the members on the basis of their patronage.

Patronage is defined differently in different types of cooperatives. For example, in a marketing cooperative patronage is based on the dollar volume bought or sold by the member through the cooperative. A worker cooperative is a cooperative where the members are the people working in the company, and where patronage is based on their labor as measured by hours or by pay. Thus a *worker cooperative* is a company where the membership rights, the voting rights and the profit rights, are assigned to the people working in the company—with the voting always on a one-person/one-vote basis and the profit allocation on the basis of labor patronage.

Traditional Worker Stock Cooperatives

The most controversial feature of cooperative structure is the treatment of the third set of rights, the net asset rights. How do the members recoup the value of retained earnings that adds to the net asset value? Some cooperatives treat the net asset value as "social property" that cannot be recouped by the members (see the section below on common-ownership firms). Other cooperatives used a stock mechanism for the members to recoup their capital. In the United States, the best known examples of these worker stock cooperatives are the plywood cooperatives in Oregon and Washington (see Berman, 1967 and Bellas, 1972).

The plywood cooperatives use one legal instrument, the membership share, to carry both the membership rights (voting and net income rights) *and* the member's capital rights. A worker must buy a membership share in order to be a member, but the worker only gets one vote even if he or she owns several shares. Moreover, the dividends go only to the members but are based on their labor patronage. In a successful plywood co-op, the value of a membership share could rise considerably. For example, in a recent plywood co-op "offer sheet," membership shares were offered for $95,000 with a $20,000 down payment. New workers often do not have the resources or credit to buy a membership share so they are hired as non-member employees, which recreates the employer–employee relationship between the member and non-member workers.

When the original cohort of founding workers cannot sell their shares upon retirement, the whole cooperative might be sold to a capitalist firm to finance the founders' retirement. Thus the worker stock cooperatives tend to revert to capitalist firms either slowly (hiring more non-members) or quickly (by sale of the company). Jaroslav Vanek has called them "mule firms" since they tend not to reproduce themselves for another generation.

In a democratic labor-based firm, the membership rights (voting and profit rights) are partitioned away from the net asset or capital rights, and the membership rights become personal rights attached to the workers as workers. A new social invention, the Mondragon-type internal capital accounts, is used to carry the capital rights of the members. The mistake in the stock cooperatives is that they use *one* instrument, the membership share, to carry *both* the membership and capital rights. The new workers who qualify for membership based on their labor nevertheless cannot just be "given" a membership share (carrying the membership rights) since that share *also* carries essentially the capital value accruing to any retiring member.

With the system of internal capital accounts, a new worker can be given membership (after a probationary period such as six months) but his or her account starts off at zero until the standard membership fee is paid in (for example, more like one or two thousand dollars than $95,000). The firm itself pays out the balances in the capital accounts either in cash or in negotiable debt instruments such as consols or participating debt securities.

Since the workers do not acquire membership based on their labor in these traditional worker stock cooperatives, they are not labor-based democratic firms. They represent a confused combination of capitalist features (membership based on share ownership) and cooperative attributes (one vote per member).

Common-Ownership Firms in England

A labor-based democratic firm is a firm that assigns the membership rights (the voting and residual rights) to the functional role of working in the firm. But there are two different ways to treat the third rights, the right to the net asset value. Some democratic firms treat the net asset value completely as social or common property, while other democratic firms treat it as partially individualized property.

The common-ownership firms in the UK or the Yugoslavian self-managed firms are examples of worker-managed firms which treat the net asset value as common or social property. These firms do assign the membership rights to the functional role of working in the firm, but deny any individual recoupable claim on the fruits of past labor reinvested in the firm. Most of the worker cooperatives in the United Kingdom today are organized as common-ownership cooperatives.

There are a number of problems with the social property or common-ownership equity structure which can be resolved using the Mondragon-type individual capital accounts. We consider here some of the problems in Western firms with this social property equity structure. The related difficulties in the Yugoslav self-managed firms will be considered later.

The "common-ownership" equity structure has some rather curious ideological support in the United Kingdom. Having a recoupable claim on the net asset value of the company is considered as illicit in some circles. The reason is far from clear. Perhaps the antipathy is to a capital-ist equity structure where the membership rights are treated as "capital." But then the antipathy should not extend (as it often does) to the Mondragon-type cooperative structure where the membership rights are personal rights attached to the functional role of working in the company.

Perhaps there is a lack of understanding that the only capital-based appreciation on the capital accounts is interest which has always been allowed in cooperatives. The only other allocations to the capital accounts are the labor-based patronage allocations, but those allocations are analogous to depositing a wage bonus in a savings account. A deposited wage bonus increases the balance in the savings account but it is not a return to the capital in the account. An internal capital account is a form of internal debt capital. Apparently there is no general antipathy in common-ownership companies to workers having explicit debt claims on retained cash flows. The largest common-ownership company, the John Lewis Partnership, has "paid out" bonuses in debt notes to be redeemed in the future. The total of the outstanding debt notes for each member would be a simple form of an internal capital account.

The social property equity structure is best suited to small, labor-intensive, service-oriented cooperatives. None of the complications involved in setting up, maintaining, and paying out internal capital accounts arise since there are no such accounts. Since there is no recoupable claim on retained earnings, the incentive is to distribute all net earnings as pay or bonuses, and to finance all investment with external debt. But any lender, no matter how sympathetic otherwise, would be reluctant to lend to a small firm which had no incentive to build up its own equity and whose members had no direct financial stake in the company.

Firms which have converted to a common-ownership structure after becoming well-established (e.g. Scott Bader Commonwealth or the John Lewis Partnership in England) can obtain loans based on their proven earning power, but small startups lack that option. Thus the use of the common property equity structure in small co-ops will unfortunately perpetuate the image of worker cooperatives as "dwarfish," labor-intensive, under-financed, low-pay marginal firms.

The system of internal capital accounts in Mondragon-type cooperatives is not a panacea for the problems of the worker cooperatives. But it does represent an important lesson in how worker cooperatives can learn from their past experiences to surmount their problems, self-inflicted and otherwise.

Mondragon-type Worker Cooperatives

The Mondragon Group of Cooperatives

The Mondragon worker cooperatives in the Basque region of Northern Spain provide one of the best examples of worker cooperatives in the world today. The first industrial cooperative of the movement was established in 1956 in the town of Mondragon. Today, it is a complex of around 106 industrial cooperatives with more than 20,000 members which includes the largest producers of consumer durables (stoves, refrigerators, and washing machines) in Spain and a broad of array of cooperatives producing computerized machine tools, electronic components, and other high technology products. The cooperatives grew out of a technical school started by a Basque priest, Father Jose Arizmendi. Today, the school is a Polytechnical College which awards engineering degrees.

The financial center of the Mondragon movement is the Caja Laboral Popular (CLP), the Bank of the People's Labor. It is a cooperative bank with 180 branch offices in the Basque region of Spain. The worker cooperatives, instead of the individual depositors, are the members of the Caja Laboral Popular. The bank built up a unique Entrepreneurial Division with several hundred professionally trained members. This division has in effect "socialized" the entrepreneurial process so that it works with workers to systematically set up new cooperatives (see Ellerman, 1984a). The division is now split off as a separate cooperative, *Lan Kide Suztaketa* or LKS.

The CLP is one of a number of second-degree or superstructural cooperatives which support the activities of the Mondragon group. There is also:

— *Arizmendi Eskola Politeknikoa,* a technical engineering college which was the outgrowth of the technical school originally set up by Father Arizmendi;
— *Ikerlan,* an advanced applied research institute that develops applications of new technologies for the cooperatives (for example CAD/CAM, robotics, computerized manufacturing process control, and artificial intelligence);
— *Lagun-Aro,* a social service and medical support cooperative serving all the cooperators and their families in the Mondragon group; and
— *Ikasbide,* a postgraduate and professional management training institute.

The whole Mondragon cooperative complex has developed in a little over 30 years. It has pioneered many innovations, including the system of internal capital accounts. A worker's account starts off with the paid-in membership fee, it accrues interest (usually paid out currently), and it receives the labor-based allocation of retained profits and losses. Upon termination, the balance in a worker's account is paid out over several years. There is also a collective account which receives a portion of retained profits or losses. The collective account is not paid out; it is part of the patrimony received by each generation of workers and passed on to the next generation (for more analysis, see Oakeshott, 1978; Thomas and Logan, 1982; Ellerman, 1984a; Wiener and Oakeshott, 1987; or Whyte and Whyte, 1988).

Implementing the Mondragon-type Co-op in America

A *Mondragon-type worker cooperative* is a labor-based worker cooperative with a system of internal capital accounts. There are several ways to implement this legal structure in the United States. A firm can incorporate under standard business corporation law and then internally restructure as a Mondragon-type worker cooperative using a special set of by-laws (e.g. ICA, 1984).

The key to the by-law restructuring of a standard business corporation as a Mondragon-type worker cooperative is to partition the conventional bundle of ownership rights attached to the shares so that the membership rights can be transformed into personal rights assigned to the workers. Since the net asset rights need to be partitioned off from the membership rights, two instruments are required (unlike the one membership share in the traditional stock cooperatives). Thus either the net asset rights or the membership rights must be removed from the equity shares in the restructured business corporation. The net asset rights are separated off from the shares, and kept track of using another mechanism than share ownership, namely, the internal capital accounts.

After a probationary period (typically six months), an employee must be accepted into membership or let go (the "up or out rule"). If accepted, the worker is issued one and only one share, the "membership share." Membership has obligations as well as rights. Just as a citizen pays taxes, so a member is required to pay in a standard membership fee usually out of payroll deductions. This forms the initial balance in the member's internal capital account. When the member retires or otherwise terminates work in the company, the membership share is forfeited back to the firm. The person's internal account is closed as of the end of that fiscal year, and the closing balance is paid out over a period of years.

The by-laws require that the membership share is not transferable to anyone else. The company issues it upon acceptance into membership, and the company takes it back upon termination. Since the share is not marketable, it has no market value. It functions simply as a value-less *membership certificate*. Having two membership shares would give one no more rights than having two ID cards or two identical passports. One would just be a copy of the other. In this manner, the allocation of the shares is transformed from a property rights allocation mechanism (whoever buys the shares) to a personal rights allocation mechanism (assigned to the functional role of working in the firm beyond the probationary period).

Since the value has been stripped away from the share-as-membership-certificate, the internal capital accounts are created to take over that function of recording the value to be ultimately paid back to the member. That value balance remains a property right representing the value of the members' paid-in membership fees, the reinvested value of the fruits of their labor, and the accumulated interest. If a member dies, the membership rights (as personal rights) revert to the firm while the balance in the person's capital account would be paid out to the person's estate and heirs.

In America, corporations are chartered by state law, not federal law, so there are fifty state corporate statutes. The cooperative by-laws could be used in a business corporation in any of the states. However, some states have now passed special statutes for Mondragon-type cooperatives using internal capital accounts. The first worker cooperative statute in America explicitly authorizing the Mondragon-type system of internal capital accounts was codrafted by ICA attorney Peter Pitegoff and the author, and was passed in Massachusetts in 1982 (see Ellerman and Pitegoff, 1983). Since then, mirror statutes have been passed in a number of other states [Maine, Connecticut, Vermont, New York, Oregon, and Washington as of 1989]. Similar legislation is being prepared for other states. A British version of the statute has been accepted in Parliament as Table G of the Companies Act.

Risk Diversification and Labor Mobility

There are two conventional arguments against worker owner-ship that need to be considered in light of the Mondragon experience. One argument is that worker ownership impedes the birth and death of firms by cutting down on labor mobility. The other argument is that worker ownership forces the workers to bear too much risk since they cannot diversify their capital in a large number of enterprises.

Both arguments tend to assume that the approach to these problems in a capitalist economy is the only approach. For instance, labor mobility—by contracting or closing some firms and starting or expanding others—is not the only mechanism of industrial change. In Mondragon, management planning takes the membership in the firm as a given short-run fixed factor not under the discretionary control of the management (see Ellerman, 1984b). When a business is failing in its current product line, the response is not to contract the firm by firing workers. The response is to convert the business in a deliberate manner to a more profitable line. The crucial element in the conversion is the socialization of entrepreneurship through the CLP's Empresarial Division-LKS. The Empresarial Division-LKS uses its broad knowledge of alternative product lines to work with the managers on the conversion. Thus the social function of allowing old product lines to die and promoting new products is carried out in a manner that does not presuppose labor mobility.

The other argument is that, under worker ownership, the workers cannot reduce their risk by diversifying their equity capital holdings. Since a worker typically works in only one job, attaching equity rights to labor allegedly does not allow diversification of risk. All the worker's eggs are in one basket. But there are other ways to address the risk reduction problem, namely the *horizontal association* or grouping of enterprises to pool their business risks. The Mondragon cooperatives are associated together in a number of regional groups that pool their profits in varying degrees. Instead of a worker diversifying his or her capital in six companies, six companies partially pool their profits in a group or federation and accomplish the same risk-reduction purpose without transferable equity capital.

Suppose that with some form of transferable equity claims a worker in co-op 1 could diversify his or her equity to get (say) 50 per cent of firm 1's average income per worker and then 10 per cent each from firms 2 through 6 to make up his or her annual pay. The alternative is risk-pooling in federations of cooperatives. The six cooperatives group together so that a member gets 40 per cent of average income per worker from his or her firm plus 60 per cent of the average of all the six firms. A co-op 1 worker would receive the same diversified income package as the previous annual pay obtained with transferable equity claims. Thus transferable equity capital is not necessary to obtain risk diversification in the flow of annual worker income.

5

Employee Stock Ownership Plans

ESOPs: An American Phenomenon

After a century of unionism in America, only about 15 per cent of the nonagricultural workforce is unionized and that percentage is declining. In only a decade and a half, ESOPs have spread to cover about 10 per cent of the workforce and that percentage is climbing. Clearly something significant is happening.

Are ESOPs a revolution in industrial relations comparable to the union movement itself, or are they only a temporary tax-driven management-dominated ripoff? Although this question cannot be definitely answered at this point, there is still much to be learned from an analysis of the ESOP phenomenon.

Employee ownership has so far not become a partisan issue in America or the United Kingdom. Publications favorable to ESOPs in the UK have been recently promoted by the conservative Adam Smith Institute (Taylor, 1988) and by the Fabian Research Unit (McDonald, 1989). In America, ESOPs draw support from across the relatively narrow political spectrum. While there is strong conservative support for ESOPs, the right wing in America has not been a strong supporter of worker empowerment. That suggests most ESOPs have not been a form of worker empowerment. Joseph Schuchert, managing partner of Kelso & Co., the top ESOP investment banking firm, is quite forthright.

> Our programs are the antithesis of workplace democracy. ...We've been criticized for not giving workers more participation, but we believe workers are natural shareholders, not natural managers. (quoted in Hiltzik, 1985, p. 54)

What then does drive the current ESOP movement in the minds of conservatives and moderates?

One motive cited by conservatives and moderates is the maldistribution of wealth and income. For instance, over half of the personally-held corporate stock is held by the top one per cent of households (with similar statistics holding in the UK, see McDonald, 1989, p. 10). Conventional capitalism is characterized as a "closed-loop financing system"—in other words, the rich get richer and the poor get poorer. New wealth accrues primarily to equity ownership, so until workers get in on equity ownership, they will remain permanently outside the loop. Thus the idea is "Capitalism—Heal Thyself." ESOPs are the prescription.

The developer of the leveraged ESOP idea (see below) and the founder of Schuchert's firm, Louis O. Kelso, describes the "antithesis of workplace democracy" as *democratic* capitalism (see Kelso and Kelso, 1986). Apparently there is such pressure to use the word "democratic" in America that it has to be suitably redefined so that it can be applied to its "antithesis." The adjective "democratic" is sometimes used to mean anything that can be spread amongst the common people without discrimination—like the common cold. The wealth redistributive purpose of ESOPs is to give the common people a "piece of the action" and thus to make capitalism more "democratic" in *that* sense.

But other motives seem to have hitched a ride on the redistributive bandwagon. By investing workers with ownership, workers may be weaned away from unions. In fact many of the ESOPs designed as "the antithesis of workplace democracy" would leave workers without any form of collective decision-making and action.

Many ESOPs are set up in small to medium-sized family-owned firms which are seldom a hot-bed of unionism. The founder, or his family, want to cash out at least over a period of years. The traditional route has been to sell to a large firm—which left the loyal employees with an uncertain fate. The alternative of getting tax breaks by selling to the workers through an ESOP is thus motivated by a tax-sweetened paternalism. ESOP consultants sometimes use the pitch, "Here is how you can sell your company and still keep control of it."

In the current takeover atmosphere, large firms are turning to ESOPs for rather different reasons. With an ESOP, a sizable block of shares is in friendly hands so a hostile takeover is that much more difficult. The recent court decision supporting Polaroid's "instant ESOP" to defend itself against a hostile takeover bid is already leading to a host of new ESOPs that seem aimed at thwarting takeovers.

The current takeover binge seems driven less by real efficiency gains than by the short-term profits obtained by redrafting in the company's favor all the implicit contracts with the employees, the (non-junk) bondholders, and the local communities. The long-terms effects are anti-investment; they work against company investment in employee training or in new product development, against the investment of non-junk long-term capital, and against state and local government investment in infrastructure development for (now outside-controlled) companies.

Some unions have embraced ESOPs, but only after a shotgun marriage. The long-term decline of the unionized steel industry has forced workers to take their fate more and more into their own hands. The success of Weirton Steel, a 100 per cent ESOP buyout from National Steel, has been one of the brightest spots in employee ownership during recent years. Weirton has an independent union, but the United Steel Workers of America nevertheless got the message. If you have to make concessions in a declining industry, you might as well take stock rather than nothing in return for the givebacks.

Unions have found common cause with management on using ESOPs as an anti-takeover device. If the company is going to become heavily leveraged to prevent a takeover (e.g. to buy back shares), then the employees might as well be earning shares for themselves as they tighten their belts to pay off the company debt.

Employee ownership offers American liberals an almost unique opportunity to be pro-worker without being anti-business. We are witnessing the drawing to a close of the era of America's economic prominence based on the vitality of its market economy and its endowment of unexploited natural resources in the New World. In the finely-tuned competitive environment of today's international marketplace, American industry can ill-afford the inherent "X-inefficiency" of the firm organized on the basis of the us-vs.-them mentality of the employer–employee relationship (see Tomer, 1987). A new cooperative and participative model of the enterprise is needed where the workers are seen as long-term "members" rather than as "employees." Many forward-looking American liberals and progressives see worker ownership as the natural legal framework for that new model of the enterprise.

There have thus been many reasons for the ESOP phenomenon and for the widespread political support. To further analyze the ESOP contribution, we must turn to a closer description of ESOPs.

Worker Capitalist Corporations

A *worker-capitalist corporation* is a company where the conventional ownership bundle remains as a bundle of property rights, that is, as capital (not partially restructured as personal rights) and those property rights are owned by the employees of the corporation. Instead of directly working for themselves, the workers own the capital that employs them.

In a worker-capitalist firm, the employee might own the shares directly or only own them indirectly through a trust such as an Employee Stock Ownership Plan or ESOP. Before considering these two forms, it should be noted how worker-capitalist firms violate the democratic rule of one vote per person and do not allocate the net income in accordance with labor.

Votes are conventionally attached to shares, and different employees will usually own widely differing numbers of shares (different longevity, pay rates, and so forth). The votes will be as unequal as the share distribution. The voting rights are part of the property rights attached to the shares so it is the shares that vote, not the people. The shareholders don't vote themselves; they vote their shares.

In any capitalist firm, worker-owned or absentee-owned, the net income ultimately accrues to the shareholders either in the form of share dividends or capital gains (increased share value). Both dividends and capital gains are per share so they are proportional to the shareholding of the employees, not their labor during the fiscal year.

Before the development of ESOPs, there were sporadic examples of worker buyouts that established worker capitalist firms where the workers directly owned all or a majority of the shares. When the shares are *directly* owned by some or all of the employees, the employee ownership tends to be a very temporary characteristic of the company—at least in a full-blown market society. If the company succeeds, the share value rises so the workers and their shares are soon parted. The Vermont Asbestos Group and the Mohawk Valley Community Corporation were examples of pre-ESOP worker buyouts in the 1970s. Within three to five years, managers or outsiders had purchased majority control in both companies.

Employee-owned corporations are more stable if the shares are *indirectly* owned through a trust as in the employee stock ownership plans (ESOPs). In an ESOP, each employee has an account which keeps track of the employee's capital. The shares represented in the accounts are held in the trust so the employees cannot sell them. The employees only receive the shares upon leaving the company or retirement, and even then the company usually buys back the shares to maintain the employee-owned nature of the company.

In a conventional ESOP, the voting and profit rights are distributed to workers—not according to their labor—but according to their capital. The voting is on one per share basis, and workers and managers can own widely differing numbers of shares depending on their pay scale and longevity with the company. The profits accrue to the employee-shareholders either as dividends or as capital gains (realized increase in share price) and both are proportional to the number of shares held, not the labor performed by the worker.

Origin of ESOPs

The original architect of the ESOP was a corporate and invest-ment banking lawyer, Louis Kelso, who has co-authored books entitled *The Capitalist Manifesto, How to Turn Eighty Million Workers Into Capitalists on Borrowed Money,* and *Two-Factor*

Theory. The conservative but populist aspects of the Kelso plan appealed to Senator Russell Long (son of spread-the-wealth Southern populist, Huey Long), who pushed the original ESOP legislation through Congress and continued to spearhead the ESOP legislation (e.g. the *Tax Reform Act of 1984*) until his recent retirement from the Senate.

An ESOP is a special type of benefit plan authorized by the Employee Retirement Income Security Act (ERISA) of 1974. As in any employee benefit plan, the employer contributions to an ESOP trust are deductible from taxable corporate income. But, unlike an ordinary pension trust, an ESOP invests most or all of its assets in the employer's stock. This makes an ESOP into a new vehicle for worker ownership but a poor substitute for a normal pension plan since it is not diversified.

ESOPs have received strong tax preferences so for that reason, if for no other, their growth has been significant. From the beginning in 1974, 10,000 ESOPs sprung up in the United States covering about 10 per cent of the workforce (in comparison, about 15 per cent of the workforce is unionized). There are perhaps 1000 ESOPs holding a majority of the shares in the company. However, only 50–100 of the ESOPs have the democratic and cooperative attributes such as one-person/one-vote as opposed to one-share/one-vote. The overwhelming majority of ESOPs are designed by managers to be controlled by management and the lenders (at least for the duration of the ESOP loan).

The main tax advantage to the company is the ability to deduct the value of shares issued to an ESOP from the taxable corporate income. The *Tax Reform Act of 1984* has increased the tax-favored status of ESOPs for companies, owners, and banks. The taxable income to a bank is the interest paid on a bank loan. On a loan to a leveraged ESOP, 50 per cent of the interest is now tax-free to the bank. Dividends paid out on stock held in an ESOP are deductible from corporate income (similar to an existing tax benefit of cooperatives) whereas dividends in conventional corporations come out of after-tax corporate income. If an owner sells a business to an ESOP (or a worker-owned cooperative) and reinvests the proceeds in the securities of another business within a year, then the tax on the capital gains is deferred until the new securities are sold. These tax breaks have made the ESOP into a highly favored financial instrument.

Due to the strong tax preferences to the firms as well as to lenders, most large-sized worker-owned companies in the United States are organized as ESOPs. However, the transaction costs involved in setting up and administering an ESOP are large, so the cooperative form is often used for smaller worker-owned enterprises. The ESOP structure allows for partial employee ownership—whereas a cooperative tends to be an all-or-nothing affair. Indeed, most ESOPs are hybrid companies which combine employee with absentee ownership. The average ESOP company has less than 20 per cent employee ownership (for a review of the ESOP literature and research, see Blasi, 1988).

Structure of ESOP Transactions

In the leveraged ESOP transaction, the corporate employer adopts an employee stock ownership plan (ESOP) which includes a trust as a separate legal entity formed to hold employer stock. The ESOP borrows money from a bank or other lender (step ① in Figure 5.1), and uses that money to purchase some or all of the employer stock at fair market value (steps ② and ③). The loan proceeds thus pass through the trust to the employer, and the stock is held in the trust. Ordinarily, the company guarantees repayment of the loan by the ESOP and the stock in the trust is pledged to guarantee the loan.

Over time, the employer makes contributions of cash to the ESOP in amounts needed to repay the principal and interest of the bank loan (step ④) and the trust passes the payments through to the bank (step ⑤). Thus, the employer pays off the loan gradually by repayments to the lender through the ESOP—payments that are deductible from taxable income as deferred labor compensation. This deduction of both interest and principal payments represents a significant tax advantage since the employer ordinarily can deduct only the interest payments. The implicit cost of the tax break to the original shareholders is the dilution of their shares represented by the employee shares in the ESOP.

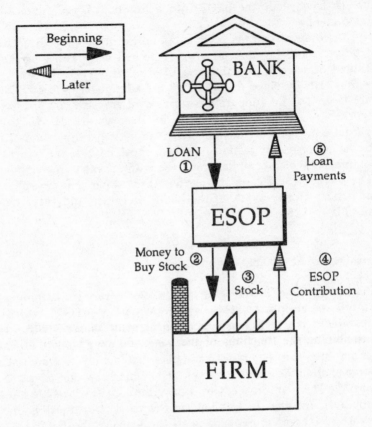

Figure 5.1 A Standard Leveraged ESOP

An ESOP can also be used to partially or wholly buy out a company from a private or public owner. This is called the "leveraged *buyout* transaction." Taking the previous owner as the government, the ESOP borrows money (step ① in Figure 5.2) and the loan payments are guaranteed by the firm with the purchased shares as collateral. The shares are then purchased from the owner, the government, with the loan proceeds (steps ② and ③)—instead of buying newly issued shares from the company.

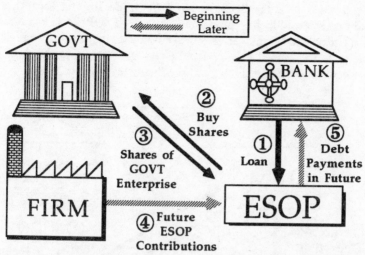

Figure 5.2 Leveraged Worker Buy-Out of Government Enterprise

Again the firm makes ESOP contributions which are passed through to pay off the loan (steps ④ and ⑤). A variation on this plan is for the seller to supply all or some of the credit. By combining the functions of the bank and government in the above diagram, we have the "pure credit" leveraged buyout transaction.

ESOPs in the United Kingdom

Prior to the 1989 Budget, the United Kingdom had no legislation specifically for ESOPs, i.e. for tax-favored leveragable trusts which can hold all or some of the shares in the employer. However, the virtual equivalent of the basic ESOP arrangement could be constructed using two different kinds of trusts. A firm can make tax deductible contributions to a 1978 share scheme to purchase shares, but such a share scheme cannot take out loans. Hence another type of trust, a closed market trust, is used to take out the loan and originally purchase shares from the company. In the UK, "ESOP" is usually taken to stand for Employee Share (instead of Stock) Ownership Plan.

The Unity Trust Bank, owned by trade unions and the Cooperative Bank, has pioneered this UK ESOP arrangement. The Unity Trust Bank (or any other financial institution) makes a loan to the closed market trust (step ①) which uses the loan proceeds to purchase stock from the firm (steps ② and ③).

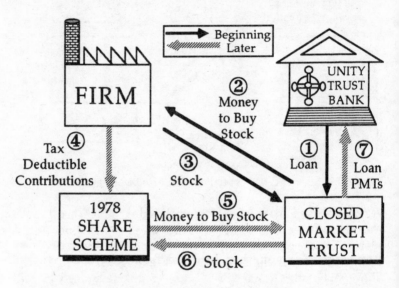

Figure 5.3 UK ESOP Arrangement

Over the duration of the loan, the firm makes tax deductible contributions to the 1978 share scheme (step ④), which in turn purchases the shares from the closed market trust (steps ⑤ and ⑥)—which in turn pays off the loan to the bank (step ⑦).

The Unity Trust Bank has used the ESOP arrangement in companies such as Roadchef, Peoples Provincial Buses, Coventry Pressworks, and Llanelli Radiators. There are around 15 companies in the UK using an ESOP-type arrangement. In the 1989 Budget, Government gave official approval for the tax deductibility of the contributions used by pay off the ESOP loan, a tax break that had been previously challenged by the Inland Revenue.

Two Examples of ESOPs

The American steel industry is one of the industries hardest hit by foreign competition. One of the brightest spots in the industry is a 100 per cent employee-owned (but not presently employee-controlled) company, *Weirton Steel*, in Weirton, West Virginia. Using borrowed money and taking a wage cut, the employees purchased the company in 1984 from a conglomerate which wanted out of the steel industry. Since the buyout, worker productivity has increased, worker participation and involvement programs have been successfully implemented, and profits have been quite good. It is currently producing about 2 million tons a year of continuous cast tin plate with over 7000 employee-owners.

On a smaller scale (230 workers) in Seymour Connecticut, the *Seymour Specialty Wire Company* has been a successful worker buyout from a conglomerate leaving the metals industry. Seymour Specialty Wire is one of the largest democratic ESOPs in the country. The employees elect the entire Board of Directors on a one vote per worker basis. Since the buyout four years ago, Seymour has profited from increased worker productivity and involvement—although it has not escaped the ups and downs of a medium-sized manufacturing company in a declining sector.

Democratic ESOPs

Voting in a Democratic ESOP

Can an ESOP be restructured to approximate a democratic firm, a democratic ESOP? In a conventional ESOP, the capital account is kept in terms of shares (share-denominated accounts) rather than in terms of value (value-denominated accounts as in the Mondragon-type capital accounts). There is also a suspense account which is a temporary collective account holding ESOP shares as yet unallocated to the individual share accounts. Usually the votes on the shares in an employee's account are not "passed through" to the employee in a corporation without publicly traded shares. Even when the vote is passed through, it is on a one-share/one-vote basis, and the employees do not vote the ESOP shares in the suspense account.

There is, however, a voting arrangement for American ESOPs that gives democratic voting of all ESOP shares both in the employee accounts and in the suspense account. The votes are not passed through. Instead, a side election is held on a one-person/one-vote basis to instruct the trustee how to vote all the ESOP shares. This is called the "instructed trustee" model, and it has been expressly authorized in the 1986 Tax Reform Act.

Internal Capital Accounts in a Democratic ESOP

Having one vote per member is only "half" of what makes an ESOP democratic; the legal structure should also implement the principle that labor has hired capital so the residual profit (after interest) is allocated according to labor.

How are shares typically allocated to the individual employee accounts? One common arrangement is to allocate shares from the suspense account to the employee accounts at the same time and in the same amounts as the principal payments on the loan. It is as if the principal payments were distributed as a labor bonus (tax deductible to the firm and currently tax-free to the workers) and then immediately paid back in for shares in the workers' accounts. While that principal payment is usually allocated between the accounts in accordance with pay (one measure of labor), the year-end profits and losses are automatically allocated by capital gains or dividends, i.e. in a capital-based manner.

A democratic ESOP could follow the Mondragon-type allocation rule that allocates profits (after interest) to the employee accounts in accordance with labor (since it is structured according to the principle of labor hiring capital). The ESOP trust would have to be restructured with value-denominated accounts and a Mondragon-type allocation rule.

It is also possible to have a membership fee in an American democratic ESOP. This is accomplished by making the ESOP "contributory" in the sense that employee out-of-pocket payments or payroll deductions purchase shares which are

116

credited to their ESOP capital accounts (for more analysis of democratic ESOPs, see Pitegoff, 1987).

It is of some importance to note that almost all ESOPs are not contributory. The workers do not pay in any money out of their pockets (although ESOPs in distressed firms usually involve pay cuts). In fact, workers play an almost completely passive role in the establishment of most ESOPs—and that seems to be part of the implicit contract that results in management-dominated ESOPs. Management, in effect, offers the shares to the workers "for free" (in the sense of no out-of-pocket money) in return for the workers letting the managers control the ESOP. Management senses that if workers made tangible sacrifices to obtain the stock, then the workers are going to demand full exercise of their rights.

ESOPs and Cooperatives

What advantages do ESOPs have over worker cooperatives? We must first set aside legislated incentives enjoyed exclusively by ESOPs which play no role in structural comparisons of ESOPs and worker co-ops. Under present American legislation, some tax benefits apply to both ESOPs and worker cooperatives while some apply only to ESOPs. For instance, for bank loans to ESOPs, but not to worker cooperatives, 50 per cent of the interest paid back to the bank is excluded from the bank's taxable income.

The major advantage of the ESOP legal structure seems to be as a vehicle for *partial* worker ownership. A cooperative is not easily hybridized; it is usually an all or nothing affair. The immediate implementation of a full cooperative assumes the eventual goal—a workforce ready and able to take democratic control of their workplace—at the very outset. A partial transitional legal structure is needed to gradually build up to full democratic worker ownership. An ESOP can play that role.

While the ESOP has filled a structure gap in the American legal context, ESOP law has evolved in a rather haphazard and idiosyncratic manner. Other countries considering worker ownership legislation should rethink the desired ownership structure and legislate creatively—rather than simply mimicking American ESOP law. For instance, the American ESOP uses a separate trust and the UK ESOP uses two separate trusts, but the basic idea of the ESOP transaction can be implemented as a part of the corporate law without any separate trust. That is particularly important for countries that have no appropriate trust law. The *hybrid democratic firm* described in later chapters uses the internal trust model to combine the best from the experience with ESOPs and the Mondragon-type worker cooperatives.

6
ESOP Analysis and Evaluation

The Ideology of the ESOP Movement

ESOPs are certainly touted as "worker capitalism"—although the reality is interestingly different from the advertisements. But first we should consider the ideologies surrounding ESOPs.

The originator and popularizer of the leveraged ESOP is Louis Kelso. Kelso's "two-factor theory" is particularly bizarre. When today's economists talk about "productivity," they are referring to *labor* productivity. Kelso apparently inferred that capitalist economists think that labor is the only productive factor (never mind over à century of criticism of the labor theory of value by the same capitalist economists). Kelso has discovered another productive factor, capital, so there are really two productive factors, labor and capital. Kelso announced this discovery in a book *Two-Factor Theory* (Kelso and Hetter, 1967), and, to this day, he refers to his theories as "Binary Economics" (see Kelso, 1988a).

How does all this relate to ESOPs? Kelso claims that capital is much more productive than labor, and that if labor was really paid according to its productivity, the workers would not receive a living wage. Thus the economy is askew; labor is being paid more than it is worth so that workers can survive, and capital is underpaid. Kelso's solution is to give workers a capital income, to make them "capital workers" in addition to labor workers. Then labor and capital can each be paid what they are worth, workers will do well on their two incomes, and the economy will finally be set aright.

To professional economists, Kelso's theories have all the earmarks of a self-taught credit-crank, and they treat him accordingly.

119

> The U.S. today has so-called ESOP plans that give some tax loophole advantage to certain kinds of profit-sharing trusts. Louis Kelso, a San Francisco lawyer, has made extensive claims for such innovations. Often John-Law schemes, in which somehow, out of bank loans, equity is created from thin air, get involved in the profit-sharing Gospel. Those few economists who have audited the economic theories underlying the proposals and the claims made for them have generally not rendered favorable verdicts on them. I must concur in these negative appraisals. (Samuelson, 1977, n. 3, p. 16)

Indeed, anyone who announces in the twentieth century that they have discovered the productivity of capital is not likely to be met with a chorus of hosannas from the economics profession. While economists have treated the two-factor theory as beneath comment, ESOPs have nevertheless grown to cover about 10 per cent of the workforce in a decade and a half. *Something* is happening that requires attention.

In the circles of ESOP promoters, Kelso's "two-factor theory" and "binary economics" is all very politely ignored, and treated only as the idiosyncratic indulgence of the founding father of the ESOP concept. Senator Russell Long and other ESOP advocates such as Jeffrey Gates use a populist or redistributive approach. ESOPs cut workers in on a "piece of the action." ESOPs help correct the obscene maldistribution of income and wealth in America. When people get rich, it is usually through the appreciation of equity capital, not through wages and salaries. When profits are made and reinvested in companies, that accrues to the existing equity holders, and does not create any new equity owners. The ESOP changes that. Some of the reinvested profits flows to the workers through their ESOP. The workers can thus cut into the otherwise "closed-loop" financing system; some of the flow of new value is redirected to them. Since the closed-loop system exemplifies the logic of capitalism—to those who have capital, the profits shall be given—ESOPs must initially violate that logic in order to cut into the loop. This non-capitalist feature of ESOPs will be considered in the next section on the labor-based aspects of ESOPs.

Ownership of a corporation legally includes control of the corporation. The redistributive theme of cutting workers in on a piece of ownership is rather silent about cutting workers in on a proportional part of control. The ESOP movement is sometimes characterized as being "democratic" in a spread-the-wealth sense. Many of the ESOP boosters are in fact anti-democratic in the original sense of the word "democratic" pertaining to self-governance. Sometimes the whole question of workplace democracy is passed off with simplistic "Not all Indians can be chiefs" remarks as if all workers would be managers or "chiefs" in a democratic firm. That is hardly the real reason for managers' antipathy since after over two centuries of political democracy, they are well aware that democracy does not mean that "all Indians are chiefs." Rarely do those who have management power desire to be accountable—particularly to those who are managed.

There is another reason why the ESOP movement has not faced up to the real question of democracy. It is a total captive of the Fundamental Myth that governance rights are part of property ownership. ESOP ideology is the ideology of *ownership*.

One can construct an excellent political analogue by considering a government where the franchise was based on land ownership. Indeed, before the political democratic revolutions in the West, political sovereignty over people's lives was sometimes interpreted as being based on property rights in land. The monarch was the ultimate owner and ruler of the land. Some power was delegated to lesser nobilities who had "tenancy" and thus governed various regions of the country. The ownership of land was equated with political sovereignty over the people on the land. The landlord was the Lord of the land. By substituting capital for land, that interpretation of pre-democratic political government becomes one of the intellectual origins of the Fundamental Myth which interprets governance rights over workers as part of the "ownership of the means of production."

121

Given such an ownership-based system of political government, one could imagine two strategies for the transition to *political* democracy:

(1) a broadened *ownership rights* strategy, or
(2) a broadened *human rights* strategy.

In the approach of "broadened ownership" (to use a common ESOP phrase), the equation between land ownership and political sovereignty would not be challenged. Instead, the idea would be to "democratize" and broaden the ownership of land, to "give the little guy a piece of the action." By becoming small landholders, some people would then gain a small measure of political control over their lives.

In the broadened human rights approach, the idea would be to sever the connection between land ownership and political control so that the rights to govern the people residing in a community could be transformed into personal rights assigned to the functional role of residing in that community.

While there was some weakening of the grip of traditional landed property by the development of numerous small holders, the political democratic revolutions of the eighteenth and nineteenth centuries ultimately took the human rights approach and did not stop short with "broadened ownership." There are good reasons for this. The right to democratic self-determination should be a human right, not a property right which must be "purchased" from its prior "owners." From a practical viewpoint, it is a will-o'-the-wisp to think that political democracy could be approximated by keeping the rights to govern people's lives as property rights.

It is a fundamental fact that property rights can be concentrated into a few hands, while personal rights are automatically decentralized on a one-per-person basis. As long as political power was based on property ownership, it would be futile to expect the broadened ownership of small landholders to fundamentally challenge the historical concentrations of property and power. Political democracy was only established by removing the question of political sovereignty from the whole arena of property rights through universal suffrage without property qualifications.

122

That analogy captures the redistributive impulse in ESOP ideology. The redistributive impulse is well-intended. But it usually contains no clue that the road to democracy lies not in redistributing property but in separating the governance rights off from property ownership and in restructuring those rights as personal rights attached to the functional role of being governed. That is the road already taken by political democracy, and that is the road ahead for economic democracy.

Labor-based Aspects of Conventional ESOPs

Progressive ESOP commentators (including the author) have sometimes drawn an over-simplified contrast between "worker-capitalist" conventional ESOPs on the one hand, and worker cooperatives and democratic ESOPs on the other hand. Yet one of the great ironies in the ESOP phenomenon is that in spite of the constant drumbeat of worker capitalist ideology amongst conservative ESOP boosters, even the conventional ESOPs have a number of significant labor-based characteristics.

In a pure worker capitalist firm, the workers would individually own the shares and the shares would be freely salable. Some workers or managers might buy shares, other might not. The correlation between work in the firm and ownership would be "accidental." In a democratic firm, the workers hold the membership rights as personal rights inherently correlated together with work in the firm. The annual patronage is allocated to the capital accounts of the workers in accordance with their labor often as measured by wages or salary. The capital rights embodied in their internal capital accounts are built up while working in the firm and are paid off when the workers leave the firm.

In an ESOP, the shares are not individually owned as salable property; they are held in a trust. The trust prevents a worker from selling his or her shares while working in the firm. It is also not an individual decision to become an owner. As loan payments are made on an ESOP loan, the typical arrangement is for shares to be allocated to the accounts of all the currently employed workers in the firm. Moreover, the shares are usually allocated between the accounts in accordance with the workers' wages or salaries. If that initial distribution of shares was not labor-based, then capital-less workers could never cut into the closed-loop system of capitalism. And when the workers leave the firm and can then sell the shares freely, the usual arrangement is for the firm to buy back the shares.

Thus the conventional ESOP, not to mention the democratic ESOP, already implements significant parts of the legal structure of the democratic firm. This is not surprising in view of the legislative history of the ESOP. It is a variation on a pension plan. Participation in a pension plan is correlated with employment in the firm. Firms do not make pension contributions for people not working in the firm, and there are non-discrimination clauses which require that the pension contributions are not restricted to only certain workers. The shares purchased with the pension contributions are not individually salable by the workers; the shares are held in a trust. And the pension contribution for each worker is proportional to the worker's labor as measured by pay. All these labor-based characteristics of pension plans carry over to ESOPs giving them their strong labor-based flavor in spite of the "official" worker-capitalist ideology.

The labor-based characteristics of American ESOPs have given ESOPs some advantages over worker capitalist firms and even over traditional stock cooperatives. When the connection between ownership and work is accidental, then the workers and their shares are "soon parted." Worker capitalist firms that are successful don't remain worker-owned very long. Sooner or later there is a share-selling stampede and the workers sell out in favor of managers or outsiders. Thus there are few worker capitalist worker-owned companies. The ESOP in turn is rather stable. Some management-dominated ESOPs have sold out but that has been relatively rare.

The non-discriminative aspect of the ESOP also addresses another of the old problems in worker-owned companies, the degeneration into two classes of owner-workers and non-owner-workers. Traditional stock cooperatives, such as the plywood cooperatives in the Pacific Northwest, have had a degeneration problem as new workers could not afford to buy the shares of departing workers. Mondragon-type worker cooperatives in the United States are structured with membership attached to work in the firm. After a probationary period, the up-or-out rule requires that workers either be accepted into membership or have their contract terminated. But that up-or-out rule in American co-ops is typically only embedded in the by-laws, not in a state or Federal statute. Thus greed can set in and the current members can change the by-laws to close off membership to new workers. For ESOPs, the non-discrimination clause is part of Federal law.

The degeneration question is related to the old question of why more firms aren't set up as worker-owned firms in the first place. One important reason can be understood by reviewing the virtues of financial leverage. If the residual claimants of an investment project anticipate future profits resulting from more capital, they will want to raise the funds by borrowing as opposed to sharing the anticipated profits with new equity-holders. Financial leverage gears up the return of the current equity-holders.

The same logic holds for renting people as for renting capital. The employment relation is the legal instrument for human leverage. The people involved in starting up a new company of course anticipate that it will be profitable. Therefore it is in their interest to *hire* the additional people needed in the company as opposed to allowing them in as members. Thus the people who control the legal form of a new company will tend to choose the capitalist form (with themselves as the owners) instead of the democratic form of organization.

The same phenomenon can be observed in the political sphere. The leaders of successful revolutions or coups are in a position to determine the new form of government, and they rarely choose a democracy that could vote them out in a few years. Marxism has been the choice of many revolutionaries in part because it provides a covering ideology for non-democratic government. Capitalist entrepreneurs and Marxist autocrats have more in common than first meets the eye.

The Basic Contribution of the ESOP Idea

What do ESOPs do; what is their basic contribution to worker ownership? Why haven't workers previously cut into the closed-loop financing system? Workers can't just buy companies; they don't have the cash. But why can't they get the credit? Why can't they take out loans backed by the value of the assets to be purchased with the loan money? There are several reasons. If a buyout was totally leveraged in that fashion, then in the face of difficulties the workers could "walk away" with little or no loss leaving the bank to try to auction off the assets to recover on its loan. Thus banks look beyond asset value to "equity" put in by the borrowers—money that would be lost if the borrowers defaulted on the loan. Workers usually don't have that type of equity.

Moreover, the cash demands of running a business extend beyond owning the plant and equipment. They need operating capital to pay the initial expenses and salaries until the revenues start to come in. Borrowing that money may be even more difficult particularly with uncertainty about the market for the product. There is also prejudice against worker buyouts on the part of many traditional lenders ("That's not labor's role.") but it is not the deciding factor. "Banker bashing" is the easy excuse used by those who are unwilling to examine the more objective reasons why workers have traditionally had great difficulty financing buyouts.

One alternative is for the workers to only buy *part* of a company—a company that is already operating and showing profits. What is the collateral for the loan, and how will the workers make the loan payments? If the workers put up little or no equity, then the purchased stock might be the collateral. But how can workers make the loan payments? The dividend stream over the term of the loan would in general be quite inadequate to pay off the principal and interest on the loan (since stock may be valued at the discounted value of *all* future dividends). Moreover, the company can't declare greater dividends on the worker shares without paying the same on all shares. In addition, dividends are twice-taxed income, once at the corporate level and once at the individual level.

126

Some other collateral and some other method of payment is needed to pay off the loan for the worker share purchase. Here the ESOP idea makes its true contribution.

Basic ESOP Idea:
Use the borrowing power of the company itself to take out the loan to buy worker shares, and pay the loan off as a labor expense deductible from taxable corporate income.

The ESOP does address the traditional problem of the workers getting credit because the earning power of the company itself backs up the loan. And it addresses the problem of paying off the loan since the company itself pays off the loan— and with pretax income. That basic ESOP package has been further "sweetened" by additional ESOP legislation (see Blasi, 1988)—which may or may not survive future congressional efforts to reduce tax breaks.

To evaluate the uniqueness of the ESOP contribution, one might compare an ESOP with traditional benefit plans. The idea of a company increasing worker share ownership and treating it as a deductible expense is not new; that was the purpose of a stock bonus plan where deductible bonuses to the worker were paid in stock. Deductible cash contributions to a trust with the workers as beneficiaries are also not new; that occurs in the usual defined contribution pension plan. An ESOP differs from a stock bonus plan in that it can be *leveraged*; it can take out a loan to buy shares. An ESOP differs from a pension plan because it buys shares in the employer company (whereas pensions must be diversified). The leveraging feature is crucial because that makes the ESOP into a *financial* tool. Relaxing the diversification requirement allows the ESOP to be a financial tool for employee ownership (of the employer company).

Who Pays for ESOP Shares?

Worker shares and employer tax breaks? Are ESOPs totally "win-win"? Who pays for the shares in the ESOP?

The analogy or "picture" used by ESOP boosters is that of a loan that is invested in some productive project which in turn yields the cash flow to pay off the loan. By this picture, it appears that no one else pays for the shares; they are created out of pure credit and good investments. The new capital is "self-liquidating"; it pays for itself out of new profits.

This new capital is *self-liquidating*, meaning that it is designed to pay for itself out of the increased profits flowing from expanded production. What keeps most people from acquiring self-liquidating capital is lack of access to long-term credit. (Speiser, 1985, p. 429)

Kelso paints a similar picture using "in effect" metaphors.

In effect the employees are buying the stock and personally repaying the price, because from the moment that stock is purchased it is theirs. The corporation gives its guarantee to the bank that it will make a certain scheduled level of payment necessary to enable the trust to pay off its loan. These payments are, in effect, dividends which amount to a relatively full payout of the earnings of the assets represented by that stock. (Kelso, 1988b, p. 5)

But this lovely picture is inaccurate on two crucial points.

Firstly, the loan to buy the stock is not collateralized by just the stock but by the earning power of the company. It is by no means clear that earning power and loan repayment power is based on "capital" as opposed to "labor." American union leaders involved in ESOP deals have been quick to point out that their members usually must take a cut in pay and benefits (and perhaps relax the work rules). Even if employees do not take a pay cut in the beginning, lenders realize that in the event of difficulties, employees are more willing to finance debt repayments with pay cuts if *they* are the beneficiaries as in the ESOP arrangement.

Secondly the loan is not paid off by the cashflows thrown off by the stock investment; the dividend stream is quite inadequate to pay off a term loan. The company is obliged to pay off the loan with appropriately timed contributions channeled through the ESOP back to the bank. Those ESOP contributions must be made whether or not the return from the firm's investment of the loan proceeds would pay off the loan. Thus the picture of pure credit being used to finance a self-liquidating investment is only a "picture."

Another pollyanna description of the ESOP transaction is the *no-dilution argument* that there is no dilution since the shares are purchased at their full market value. This argument would be fine if the loan used to purchase the shares at their full value were paid off by a third party. But the company itself is paying off the loan to the ESOP that was used to purchase the shares.

ESOP descriptions often involve a type of "shell game" of switching between two quite different interpretations of the transaction. The front-end is described as an equity injection—a purchase of shares at full market value. And the back-end of the transaction is described as paying off a loan with pretax dollars. But if the front-end is described as shares being purchased with money borrowed by another party (the ESOP), then it should be added that the corporation itself pays off the *other* party's loan with the ESOP contributions. And if the back-end of the transaction is described by paying off a loan with pretax dollars, then it should be added that the company has *already* "paid for" the cash injection (the loan) with the transfer of shares to the ESOP. But ESOP descriptions often focus on either the front-end equity injection or the back-end tax-favored loan payments without giving the effect of the whole transaction.

The original question of "Who pays for ESOP shares?" can be answered with some precision if a number of "extreme-case" assumptions are made: the worker shares do not result in lower wages or lower wage demands; the worker shares do not lead to any increase in productivity or efficiency; the firm could have gotten the same loan on the same terms without using the ESOP; and there are no other tax or non-tax advantages associated with putting the loan through the ESOP. Under those extreme-case assumptions, the ESOP shares are paid for by the combination of *dilution* of the existing shareholders and the *tax break* associated with paying the loan off with pretax dollars (for a spreadsheet example, see Ellerman, 1989a).

Fortunately, the extreme-case assumptions usually do not hold. There are some tax breaks that apply specifically to ESOP loans in the United States so that the company usually cannot get the loan on the same terms. Sometimes ESOPs are established as part of an explicit wage concession bargain. Even more often, there seems to be implicit bargains or expectations that future wage demands will be tempered if an ESOP is installed. And lastly, there is good evidence that ESOPs do improve productivity particularly when coupled with concrete worker participation programs inside the firm (see Quarrey, Blasi, and Rosen, 1986; Blasi, 1988). The combination of these factors would decrease the part of the ESOP shares paid for by dilution of the existing owners—by increasing the tax breaks and by having the workers make a contribution through wage concessions and productivity enhancements.

Do these other factors completely counterbalance the dilution effect? In view of the rapid spread of ESOPs, one must conclude that for many firms, the dilution is either counter-balanced, or there are non-economic factors that outweigh any remaining dilutive effect such as the owners' desire to reward the workers and/or to induce the workers to more closely identify with the firm.

7

Model of a Hybrid Democratic Firm

Introduction: A Simplified Model for Transplanting

ESOPs and worker cooperatives have evolved in idiosyncratic ways in the United States and elsewhere. How can the "core" of these legal structures be introduced in rather different legal environments elsewhere in the West—not to mention in the socialist world? For instance, worker cooperatives have always been limited because they are all-or-nothing affairs. There is no intermediate stage that allows a company to ramp up to 100 per cent worker ownership over a period of years. This chapter presents a hybrid form of the Mondragon-type worker cooperative.

ESOPs do allow for that partial or hybrid intermediate structure. But the American ESOPs require an external trust in addition to the corporation, and the ESOPs developed in the United Kingdom have *two* external trusts. How can the ESOP structure be applied in non-Anglo-Saxon countries which have little or no trust law? This chapter presents the idea of an "internal ESOP" which captures the basic ideas of the leveraged ESOP transaction with *no* external trust.

The resulting models of a hybridized Mondragon-type worker cooperative and an internalized democratic ESOP turn out to be essentially the same—so *that* is the model of the *hybrid democratic firm* presented here.

A Hybrid Mondragon-type Worker Cooperative

The worker-owned cooperative has historically been an all-or-nothing creature. It tends to assume a workforce that already understands and appreciates the rights and responsibilities of democratic worker ownership. A more practical compromise is a hybrid structure that can initially accommodate less than 100 per cent or even minority worker ownership—but where that portion of worker ownership is organized on a democratic cooperative basis.

A *hybridized* Mondragon-type worker cooperative is a corporation where a certain percentage of the ownership rights is organized as a Mondragon-type worker cooperative, that is, with one vote per worker to determine total vote of workers' shares and with workers' residual allocated among them according to labor.

An Internalized Democratic ESOP

The democratic ESOP is already a hybrid structure for democratic worker ownership. Any percentage of the ownership could be in the ESOP, and that portion can be organized on a cooperative basis. However, the ESOP has evolved in an idiosyncratic way depending on the peculiarities of American law and the political process. In designing a new institutional form, it is best to think through the real function served by all the ESOP trust apparatus and then implement a streamlined version accomplishing the desired ends.

In particular, an external trust is a somewhat peculiar mechanism for *worker* ownership. The workers are, in fact, inside the firm. But an external ESOP trust is set up with the workers as beneficiaries. Then the firm issues external shares to be held by the trust.

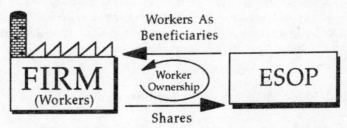

Figure 7.1   Indirect Worker Ownership Through External Trust

By this circuitous route, the workers have the ownership rights in their enterprise.

The external ESOP trust evolved in American law from a pension trust designed to hold shares in *other* companies. There is little need for the trust to be external if its primary purpose is to register ownership in the company itself. Corporate law could be modified or new corporate law drafted to, in effect, move the ESOP inside the corporation itself. The whole circuitous loop of worker ownership through an external democratic ESOP could be simplified and streamlined by moving the ESOP inside the corporation.

In America, starting and administering an ESOP requires an army of lawyers, financial analysts, valuation experts, and accountants all resulting in sizable transaction costs. Indeed, a whole industry has developed for the "care and feeding" of ESOPs. Less of this would be necessary if the ESOP structure was internal to the structure of the corporation.

An *internalized* democratic ESOP is a corporation where a certain percentage of the ownership rights is organized as a "democratic ESOP" within the company.

The Hybrid Democratic Firm

The interesting result is that a hybridized Mondragon-type worker cooperative is essentially the *same* as an internalized democratic ESOP—and *that* is the structure we are proposing as a hybrid partial worker-owned democratic firm—which, for short, will be called a *hybrid democratic firm*.

Many useful ideas can be suggested by using the two ways of conceptually deriving the structure of a hybridized democratic firm (as a hybridized co-op or an internalized ESOP). However, we will initially describe the structure in general terms.

The equity of the hybrid firm is divided into two parts:

(1) the *workers' portion of the equity* which is the "inside ownership" and

133

(2) the *external portion of the equity* owned by outside parties such as organs of government, intermediate institutions, or private parties.

In a socialist country, the external ownership might be public, that is, by the state, city, county, township, or village government.

There are two limiting cases: 0 per cent and 100 per cent inside ownership. With 0 per cent inside ownership, the firm would be a conventional corporation owned by public or private parties. With 100 per cent internal ownership, the firm would be a (non-hybridized) Mondragon-type worker cooperative which could also be seen as a 100 per cent democratic ESOP (i.e. an ESOP with 100 per cent of the ownership) internalized to the company.

In an American corporation, there is a difference between shares that are *authorized* and shares that have been issued to become *outstanding*. A certain number of shares (assume all common voting shares) are authorized in the original corporate charter. Some of these shares are then issued to shareholders in return for their paid-in capital so those shares are then outstanding. If a company bought back or redeemed any shares, those shares would not be outstanding and would be retired to the company treasury until re-issued. Only the shares that are issued and outstanding can vote or receive dividends. The authorized but unissued or redeemed shares do not vote, receive dividends, or reflect any net worth.

In what follows, we assume the hybrid firm is organized as a corporation with common voting shares—although a simpler structure might also be used to implement the ideas. In a hybrid democratic corporation with shares, the inside ownership is *a new category of issued and outstanding shares*; it is not unissued or treasury stock. The workers' stock is issued and outstanding but held in the firm for the inside owners, the workers. Each worker does not own a certain number of shares since the workers' portion of the company is to be organized in a labor-based democratic fashion. The worker *shares* are held collectively and are unmarketable. The workers vote on a one vote per worker basis as to how the collectivity of the worker shares will be voted. The workers would elect a number of representatives to the board of directors proportional to the workers' portion of the equity (e.g. one third of the directors for one third of the equity). The worker representatives on the board would form a natural subcommittee to control the shares in the workers' portion of the equity in analogy with an ESOP governing committee in the American external ESOP.

Some shares have a par or face value which is the value for which the shares were originally issued, but that value has no significance later on. Often shares are no-par shares with no par or face value; they simply have some original issued value. After a company has been in operation, the shares will have a book value (net book value divided by the number of common shares). If the shares are marketable, they will also have a market value. The book and market values are in general different from the face or issued values of the shares. The relevant valuation of the worker shares in a democratic firm is their net asset value or "economic book value" (see Ellerman, 1986b on the difference between book and market value).

Assets	Liabilities	
Cash	External Debt	

Inventory	External Equity:
	    Ext. Paid-in Capital
	    Ext. Retained Earnings
		External
		Portion
		of Equity

Equipment	Internal Equity: (Workers)	
Plant	Individual Capital Accts Suspense Account Collective Account minus Loan Balance Account	Workers' Portion of Equity = Internal ESOP

Figure 7.2   Hybrid Democratic Firm's Balance Sheet

The total book value of the worker shares is divided between three types of internal capital accounts:

(1) each worker has a value-denominated *individual capital account* which would contain a certain amount of value (not a certain number of shares);

135

(2) there is a *suspense account* which serves as a temporary collective account or "holding pen" for value to be eventually allocated to individual accounts; and possibly

(3) a permanent *collective account*. During the lifetime of an "internalized ESOP" loan, there would also be a debit-balance loan balance account which could be treated as a contra-account to the collective account.

Company law could be drafted so that the *workers' portion* of the equity was a *normal part of any corporation*. A company typically runs several accounts such as total year-to-date wages or accrued vacation time. A worker's internal capital account would be another account maintained for each person in the company.

Each worker could have a membership certificate, but it would be quite different from a share certificate. The number of shares in the total workers' portion might grow over time, but each worker only needs one membership certificate to signify membership. Each year, the workers would receive Capital Account Statements showing the transactions in their accounts due to the year's operations and the resulting ending balances.

Some details can be best illustrated by considering a concrete example. Consider a hybrid democratic firm where one-third of the ownership is inside or workers' ownership. There could be, say, 960 shares issued and outstanding with 33 per cent or 320 shares held in the firm as worker shares. In a corporate election of (say) board members, there are 960 share-votes, 320 of which are controlled by the workers. The workers vote on a democratic one vote per worker basis as to how their 320 share votes should be cast.

A new worker might pay in a standard membership fee through payroll deductions. Shares with book value equal to the membership fee would be issued by the company to the workers' portion of the equity, and that value would be credited to the new worker's individual capital account.

The workers' portion of the ownership would be exercised in not only a democratic but a labor-based manner. Workers would receive wages and salaries as usual, and then 33 per cent of the profits would be allocated among the workers according to their labor—after interest is paid on the capital accounts.

136

Profits will accrue to the workers in two ways. A firm-wide decision might be made for some of the profits to be paid out in dividends on the shares. Then, in the example, 33 per cent of the dividends would go to the workers collectively to be divided between them according to their labor (measured by pay or by hours). The dividends could be paid out in cash, or they could be added to the capital accounts and then used to pay out the oldest account entries according to the rollover plan. The remainder of the profits (not declared as dividends) would be retained so they would increase the net book value per share. The shares in the workers' portion are valued at book value. Hence 33 per cent of the retained profit (= increase in net book value) would accrue to the workers' individual accounts.

The allocation formula between worker accounts depends on whether the individual capital accounts bear interest or not. Accounting is simpler if interest is ignored, but interest is the only compensation proportional to the larger risk borne by large account holders (older workers). The interest comes out of the workers' retained profit. The interest should be added to each account with the remainder of the workers' retained profit (their one-third)—which could now be negative—allocated between the accounts according to labor. If there are little or no profits, the interest is still added to the workers' accounts and the correspondingly more negative retained profits (i.e. greater losses) are allocated between the accounts according to labor.

It should be remembered that the workers do not have any individual ownership of shares; only the book value is represented in their individual capital accounts. In the hybrid firm, the shares still package together the three main rights in the ownership bundle (voting, profit, and net asset rights). But the workers' portion of the ownership is organized in a labor-based democratic manner so the voting and profit rights (carried by the shares in the workers' portion) are split off and assigned as personal rights to the workers' role, while the book value of the worker shares is allocated between the capital accounts (individual, suspense, and collective accounts).

A worker's account would be paid out in the regular rollover payouts (assuming the rollover plan is used) with the remainder paid out after termination or retirement. There are several ways to consider the payouts on the capital accounts when the firm is a hybrid instead of 100 per cent worker-owned. If a cash payout, in accordance with the rollover plan or upon termination, is from general funds of the company (and there is no proportional payout to the external shareholders), then worker shares with book value equal to the payout should be retired to the company treasury. Alternatively, if there was a cash dividend on all shares, then the worker portion of the dividend could be credited to the accounts according to current labor and then used to rollover the oldest account entries or to pay out terminated accounts. In that case, there would be no need to retire an equal amount of shares since the external shareholders received their proportional part of the dividend payout.

The ESOP Transactions with an Internal ESOP

The "Leveraged ESOP" Transaction

Consider a hybrid firm that starts off entirely or almost entirely government-owned, e.g. in a socialist country. Then a loan is channeled through the workers' portion of the equity as an "internal ESOP" in order to increase the workers' share of the company.

Let us suppose $300,000 is borrowed by the firm from a bank. There were previously 660 shares, 640 held by the government, 20 held by the workers, and the share book value was $1,000 each. With the loan channeled through the workers' portion of the equity, 300 (= 300,000/1,000) new shares are issued to the workers' portion of the ownership so the workers then have 320/960 or 33 per cent of the ownership. However, the share value is allocated to the suspense account.

Each loan payment is divided into a principal and interest portion. In many countries such as the United States, the interest portion is already an expense deductible from taxable corporate income. The principal portion is to be treated as a labor expense so that it would also be deductible as an expense from taxable corporate income. This procedure would need to be approved by the relevant tax authorities—as it has been approved in the United States.

A value amount equal to the principal payment is allocated from the suspense account to the individual accounts to be divided between them in accordance with labor. It is *as if* each principal payment is paid out to the workers as a bonus and then immediately reinvested in worker equity, and the money is then paid to the bank as the principal payment. In this manner, the hybrid firm internally mimics the leveraged ESOP transaction.

It should be remembered that changes in the worker accounts resulting from retained profits or losses are also taking place at the end of the fiscal year in addition to the credits relating to the principal payments. Those year-end profits or losses of the firm are computed with the principal payments treated as a labor expense.

When the loan is paid off, the principal amount of the loan will have been allocated between the individual accounts. The financial reward to the whole company for channeling the loan through the "internal ESOP," the workers' portion of ownership, is that the principal payments on the loan were deducted from taxable income. The increased worker ownership should also reap other rewards through the greater motivation and productivity of the workers.

The "Leveraged ESOP" Buyout Transaction

In the previously described leveraged internal ESOP transactions, the loan money went to the company, and the worker shares were newly issued and valued at book value. An alternative leveraged transaction is to use the loan proceeds to buy externally held shares for the workers' portion of the ownership.

The bank or financial institution loans money to the company. The cash is passed through the company and used to buy back externally held shares from the government authority or other party holding the shares. However, instead of interpreting this as a share redemption (which would retire the shares to the corporate treasury), it is viewed as the workers collectively buying the shares from the external owners. Hence those shares enter the workers' portion of the ownership instead of the corporate treasury, and the workers would determine how those share votes are to be cast.

Implementation Questions

How can the hybrid democratic firm be implemented? There are questions involving both corporate structure and tax benefits. The corporate structure of the hybrid democratic firm should at best be implemented by additions to existing corporate statutes authorizing the creation of the "workers' portion" of the equity of a company. Legislation should be preceded by experimentation. The structure could be experimentally implemented (without legislation) in an enterprise by appropriately drafting the charter and by-laws of the enterprise and obtaining the agreement of the present owners and the Workers' Assembly. Starting with a joint stock company (as the "universal language" of current corporate organization), a *Model Charter* and a set of *Model By-laws* have been developed for the hybrid democratic firm (Ellerman, 1989c). These could be developed as simple amendments to existing charters and by-laws to add the workers' portion of equity onto an existing joint stock company. After the development of a model seasoned by experience in a particular country, appropriate legislation can be drafted and passed.

The tax benefits of the "internal ESOP" transactions would require authorization from the tax authorities. This requires both allowing the principal payments on loans channeled through the workers' portion of equity to be deducted as labor expenses and deferring any personal income tax incidence for the workers until the capital accounts are paid out.

There are reasonable arguments for both tax benefits as well as the strong American precedent. It is as if the principal payment was paid out as a deductible labor bonus and then immediately rolled over into equity shares in the company (the equity injection then being used to pay off the loan). Or one could think of the company as making the principal payment directly to the bank and simultaneously issuing an equal (book value) amount of shares to the workers' portion of the equity as a deductible stock bonus. In either case, it should be a deductible labor expense to the firm. The workers have no increase in their disposable income so it is reasonable to defer personal taxation until the capital accounts are paid out.

ESOPs use American trust law. Trust law tends to be quite different, idiosyncratic, or non-existent in other countries. Rather than have the costly and bulky apparatus of the external ESOP trust as in current American law, the internal or workers' portion of the equity should be a *normal part of every company*—with the workers' percentage of ownership varying from the beginning of 0 per cent up to 100 per cent.

Management and Governance Structures

We turn now to some structural aspects of management (top-down use of delegated authority) and governance (bottom-up delegation of authority) in a democratic firm (hybrid or 100 per cent).

The usual governance structure in a corporation is for the shareholders to elect the board of directors, and then for the board to appoint the general manager and possibly other members of the top management team. Top management then appoints the middle managers who, in turn, select the low-level managers or foremen at the shop floor level. In a hybrid democratic firm, the workers should elect a portion of the board at least equal to their portion of the ownership.

Even in a majority or 100 per cent worker-owned company, it is not appropriate for workers to directly elect shopfloor managers. Those managers would then be in an intolerable position between middle management and the workers. They would have to "serve two masters"—to carry out the orders and management plans from above while at the same time being answerable to the workers who elect them.

Worker-owners also should not have the right to countermand management orders at the shopfloor level (except in the case of direct physical endangerment). There must be channels for workers to use to register their complaints. These could take two forms: (1) *disagreements* over policy questions or (2) *grievances* against managers or other workers for allegedly breaking enterprise rules.

For the workers to intelligently use their ultimate control rights (e.g. votes to elect representatives to the board or to vote on other issues put to the shareholders), they must have a flow of *information* about the company operations. In particular, worker representatives need timely information in order to have an input in management decisions. There should be a number of forums where information can be communicated, questions can be asked of management, and disagreements can be expressed.

There is the *annual meeting* of the Workers' Assembly but that can only deal with the larger issues of overall policy. There should be frequent *shop meetings* (weekly, bi-weekly, or at least monthly). It is important that at least part of each meeting is not chaired by the shop foreman or any other representative of management. There should be another non-managerial elected shop or office representative such as a "shop steward." In part of the shop meetings, the shop steward should preside, disagreements should be voiced in a respectful manner (perhaps by the steward) without fear of recriminations, and the shop managers should have to explain actions and decisions which are called into question.

Another forum for communication and discussions could be the *company newsletter* or newspaper. Ordinarily, this would be controlled by management. But there should be a column given over to the shop stewards who collectively want to bring an issue before the company as a whole. There could also be letters to the editor, questions to managers with their answers, and brief interviews with randomly selected workers on the topics of current interest.

There should also be a *grievance procedure* for workers who feel they have been wronged by managers in terms of the company rules, regulations, and policies. The shop steward would function as the spokesperson for the worker with the grievance (who may otherwise be intimidated by the whole procedure). The political doctrine of "separation of powers" argues that abuses of power are best held in check if there is some separation of powers and authority between the different branches of government such as the legislative, executive, and judicial branches. The board of directors is the legislative branch and the management team is the executive branch in a company. A separate judicial branch would be an elected grievance committee that would function as the court of last appeal in the grievance procedure. However, since the grievance committee would be elected by the shareholders, the board of directors could also play that role as the court of last appeal. That would involve some loss in the separation of powers, but it is hard to imagine a grievance committee having much autonomy if the board and management are already in agreement on an issue. If the workers were convinced that major injustices or abuses had occurred with the concurrence of their board representatives and if the workers could not wait until the annual meeting of the Workers' Assembly, then they should use a recall procedure to change their representatives on the board of directors.

One general principle in any democratic organization is that those who are not in direct positions of power should have the organizational ability to voice and discuss their concerns. This is the idea of the *"loyal opposition"* (see Ellerman, 1988b discussing the inside role of a union as the loyal opposition in a democratic firm). "Opposition" is not always the right word since the idea is not to always oppose current management but to have enough *independence* so that opposition could be voiced whenever deemed necessary. That, for example, is why there should be some worker-elected representatives, herein called "shop stewards," who are not part of management's line of command, and that is why the shop stewards should chair at least part of the shop meetings. The need for some such loyal oppositional structure is obvious when workers only have a minority ownership position in a hybrid firm, but it is also needed when workers have majority or 100 per cent of the ownership. Periodic election of directors is often insufficient to keep management accountable so the watchdog role of the oppositional structure is still needed in the majority worker-owned company.

The American ESOP is a separate external trust with its own governing committee. It sometimes has its own decisions to make—independent of company decisions. For example, the ESOP might accumulate contributed funds and use them to buy back the shares of departing workers. In the simplified hybrid structure recommended here, the ESOP is internalized as part of

143

the company so there is no separate trust with its governing committee. Nevertheless, there will be some "ESOP decisions" that are decisions of the collectivity of workers, not decisions of the board or management of the hybrid firm. The suggested structure is that the worker representatives on the board form the subcommittee to function as the *"internal ESOP" governing committee*. They would decide, for example, whether dividends would be passed through to current workers, or whether the accounts would be credited and the cash paid out to rollover the oldest account entries.

An important program in a hybrid democratic firm is the *internal education program* (see Adams and Hansen, 1987). The whole idea of being part of a democratic decision-making organization might be new to the workers. The workers might be accustomed to taking orders from an authority figure. The workers have stepped out of their subordinate "employee" role to become worker-owners in a horizontally interdependent organization. They have a whole new set of rights, responsibilities, and concerns. They need to develop skills for discussion and participation in meetings, to learn something about the business side of the enterprise, and to read simplified financial statements and capital account summaries.

Responsibility should be pushed down to the lowest feasible level through worker *participation and quality-of-working-life (QWL) programs*. Worker ownership creates the possibility of substantial increases in motivation and productivity, but it is not automatic. Ownership must be realized at the shopfloor level through worker participation in order to deliver the maximum effect on productivity.

PART III

Enterprise Reform in the Socialist World

8

Enterprise Reform in Yugoslavia and China

Introduction

These are exciting times in the socialist world. The old mold is breaking. Change is in the air.

The Western press and many Western scholars still look at the world in bipolar terms: capitalism or (state) socialism. State ownership and central planning have failed to deliver a modern economy so "socialism" is being abandoned in favor of capitalism. But the reality is more complicated. There are many "socialisms" and there are many "capitalisms." If "capitalism" means a decentralized economy of independent firms with definite property rights and interrelated by input and output markets, then that also fits certain types of "socialism."

There are two broad traditions of socialism: *state socialism* and *self-management socialism*. State socialism is based on government ownership of major industry, while self-management socialism envisions the firms being worker self-managed and not owned or managed by the government (see Horvat *et al.*, 1975).

In the United Kingdom, state socialism was represented by Sidney and Beatrice Webb and the nationalizing segment of the Labour Party, while self-management socialism was represented by the old Guild Socialists such as G.D.H. Cole (see 1920), S.G. Hobson (see 1919), and A.R. Orage, by the current segments of the Labour Party and Liberal Social Democrats emphasizing "social ownership" in the sense of worker cooperatives and other democratic firms (see McDonald, 1989).

It is a thesis of this book that an economic democracy, a market economy of democratic firms, represents a common ground for the East and West. There are forces of convergence towards that common ground from both sides. An economic democracy could be seen as the humanization and democratization of a market economy where the renting of workers is universally replaced by democratic membership in the firm. An economic democracy can also be represented as the result of decentralizing and democratizing a state socialist economy in favor of a market economy of self-managing firms.

There is, thus, another interpretation of the socialist enterprise reforms than just a slow reversion to capitalism. State socialism is slowly groping towards a self-managing socialist market economy.

> [E]verywhere in the communist world it is now admitted that nationalisation did not give working people mastery over property. One of the purposes of economic reform is to remedy this. The fashionable word is "socialisation", to be achieved by workers' self-management, or by co-operative ownership, or by the sale of a firm's shares to its employees... . (*The Economist*, March 18, 1989, p. 46)

Each country will, of course, follow its own idiosyncratic path. Our purpose is to briefly describe some of those paths.

Yugoslavian Self-Management: Pitfalls of a Pioneer

Social Property Problems

A historical discussion of the current economic reforms in the socialist world should begin with Yugoslavia (see Sacks, 1983; Estrin, 1983; or Prasnikar and Prasnikar, 1986) which from the 1950s moved from the state socialist model towards a model of self-management socialism.

> The only genuinely new model—i.e. different from the various versions of the basic Soviet-type model—already in existence, is the Yugoslav model. (Nuti, 1988a, p. 357)

Being a pioneer is not all glory; the pioneer may stumble many times like one who walks at night holding the lantern behind him—of no help to himself but illuminating the path for those who follow.

In Yugoslavia, there is no centralized command planning over production. The enterprises are embedded in factor and output markets. The workers in each enterprise elect the workers' council which, in turn, through a committee structure selects the enterprise director. Legally, the director is responsible to the workers' council and the collectivity of workers, but there are strong indirect influences from the League of Communists (the party) and/or the various levels of government. The assets of the enterprise are considered to be "social property." Even though the assets may have been built up by retained earnings (that could have been paid out as pay bonuses), the enterprise only has use rights over the assets and the workers have no individualized claim against the company for the value of those assets.

In the Yugoslav self-managed firm, the two membership rights, the control rights and the net income rights, are at least partially assigned as personal rights to the workers in the firm. The assignment of the control rights to the working collectivity of the firm is attenuated by the hegemony of the League of Communists in the surrounding social structure, e.g. in the local government. The assignment of the net income to the workers is also attenuated since the income that accrues to the workers is a function of the disposition of the income. If the income is paid out in wages and bonuses then it accrues to the workers. If, however, the income is retained in the firm, then it reverts to "social property" and the workers lose any recoupable claim on it.

The weakness in the net income rights can be traced to the treatment of the third right in the traditional ownership bundle, the rights to the value of the net assets of the firm. That right is treated as disembodied "social property." The problems in the Yugoslav economy, of course, cannot be traced to any one source. But surely one of the most important sources of malfunction has been this social property equity structure which has broad ramifications for efficiency and motivation throughout the economy.

If retained earnings become social or common property, the workers lack a long-term interest in the company. Reinvestment of earnings to buy a machine might not penalize younger or middle-aged workers who would be around to depreciate the machine. But an older worker near retirement or a worker thinking about leaving the firm would be simply losing what could otherwise be a pay bonus. Since the different responses are due to different time horizons with the firm, the original property rights deficiency is called the *"horizon problem"* of the Yugoslav firms (see Furubotn and Pejovich, 1970, 1974; Ellerman, 1986b; or Bonin and Putterman, 1987).

It might be noted parenthetically that there is a whole academic literature on what is called the "Illyrian firm" (see Ward, 1967; or Vanek, 1970) named after the Roman province that is now part of Yugoslavia. The main peculiarity of this model is that it assumes the firm would expel members when that would increase the net income of the surviving members. The resulting short-run perversities have endeared the model to capitalist economists. Yet the Illyrian model has been an academic toy in the grand tradition of much of modern economics. The predicted short-run behavior has not been observed in Yugoslavia or elsewhere, and worker-managed firms such as the Mondragon cooperatives take membership as a short-run fixed factor (see Ellerman, 1984b). Moreover, in spite of intensive academic cultivation in the Illyrian field for almost two decades, not a single practical recommendation has emerged for the structure of real world labor-managed firms— other than "Don't start acting like the Illyrian model." Hence we will continue to treat the Illyrian model with its much-deserved neglect.

The valuable analysis of the property rights deficiencies in the "social property" structure of many labor-managed firms is often packaged together with the perversities of the Illyrian model in academic literature. Yet the two are quite independent. Property rights problems arise with labor taken as a fixed factor and for a wide range of firm objectives. Unlike the Illyrian model, academic analysis of the property rights problem in labor-managed firms is an important contribution to the theory and practice of workers' self-management.

With social property, the incentive is to distribute all net earnings as pay (wages and bonuses) and to finance all investment with external debt. The resulting consumer demand and the upward push on money supply to satisfy the demand for loans will both fuel inflation—which has become a serious problem in Yugoslavia.

The social property structure also creates an unnecessary bias against bringing in new workers. Economic necessity as well as government regulation in the case of Yugoslavia will lead social property firms to retain some earnings to finance investment in firm assets (in spite of the pressure to finance all investment by borrowing). One way the workers can try to recoup "their investment" is through higher wages—which, in part, are implicit rent on the new assets. Any new workers would receive the same "wage" for the same work but would not have contributed to that investment. Allowing new workers in would be forcing the old workers to share the rent on their implicit equity. Thus the social property structure leads to a bias against new workers—who often have to find jobs as "guest workers" in Northern Europe. With the system of internal capital accounts, the old workers receive the rent or interest on their explicit account balance, that rent is not shared with new workers, and thus that forced-rent-sharing bias against new workers is removed.

In Alec Nove's guidebook on the economic reforms, *The Economics of Feasible Socialism* (1983), he notes these problems created by the Yugoslav social property structure.

Reverting to labour's role in managerial decisions in socialised enterprises, one must recall two negative aspects of Yugoslav experience. One is the interest of the workers in not expanding the labour force, at a time of serious unemployment, because to do so would reduce their incomes. The other is the lack of long-term interest of the workers in "their" enterprise, because it is in fact *not* theirs: they derive no benefit from working for it once they leave it, having no shares to sell. (Nove, 1983, p. 217)

The problems with social property equity structure can be solved using the Mondragon-type individual capital accounts.

A Decentralizing Model for Restructuring Socialist Firms

Other socialist countries, much in the press, have nevertheless barely begun to free their enterprises from their supervisory ministries, a task carried out in Yugoslavia decades ago. In the midst of its considerable nationality problems, Yugoslavia is now moving towards the next step of restructuring most of its socially owned enterprises as partly or wholly worker-owned enterprises under a new Enterprise Law was passed in 1989 which allows private closely-held limited liability companies and joint-stock corporations.

This reorganization provides the opportunity for a much needed restructuring of socialist firms. The Yugoslav economists, Tea Petrin and Ales Vahcic, have highlighted one of the problems of socialist economies in the maldistribution of firm size [Vahcic and Petrin, 1989]. One can perform an "inkblot test" to differentiate a socialist economy from a capitalist economy by observing the number of small businesses of 15 to 200 workers—firms larger than micro-businesses but smaller than medium-sized firms.

For illustrative purposes, Vahcic and Petrin consider the firms sizes that demarcate the ten percentiles of the industrial workforce in a Western economy such as Sweden.

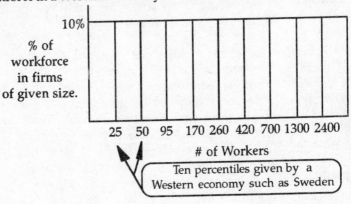

Figure 8.1 Ten Percentiles of Size Distribution of Firms

Those demarcations define the (non-linear) scale on the horizontal axis in Figure 8.1 developed by Petrin and Vahcic. Then the data from a socialist economy is displayed by graphing the percentage of workers falling in each of the same categories.

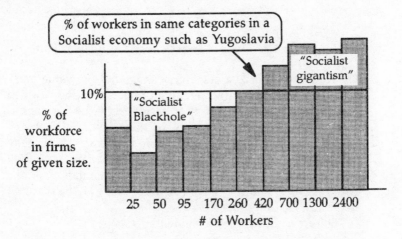

Figure 8.2 Petrin-Vahcic "Socialist Blackhole" Graph

They call the characteristic dearth of small businesses in socialist economies the *"socialist blackhole"* (physicists might insist it should be "socialist vacuum" but the meaning is clear). At the other end of the size distribution, socialist economies have their characteristic gigantism. The restructuring of ownership should be accompanied by splitting up and decentralizing the huge socialist firms so as to reduce socialist gigantism at one end of the scale and to fill the socialist blackhole at the other end. The resulting worker-owned firms should be medium-sized or small businesses that are human-scaled, more competitive, and perhaps even entrepreneurial.

The constraint on restructuring is that the value of the social property in the original firm must be maintained.

153

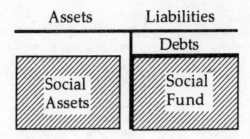

Figure 8.3 Lump of Social Property in Yugoslav Firm

The form of the social assets may change but the value must be preserved. For clarity and freedom of operation, the new democratic worker-owned firms that result from the restructuring should have no social property in them. We will sketch a restructuring model that fulfills these desiderata. The general outline of the model might be used in other socialist countries as well. The details might change with implementation since the actual legal constraints on restructuring will only be discovered as the restructuring takes place.

The restructuring can be divided into steps:

(1) The workers and managers in the original socialist firm are divided into divisions perhaps with some remaining in a central unit.

(2) The people in each division, as independent citizens, set up joint stock companies with each person making a small but mandatory contribution of cash.

(3) The same people in the Workers' Assembly of the original socialist firm then vote to convert the firm into a joint stock company and to issue its stock to the various companies set up by the divisional members in return for some of their cash. The value of the social assets is balanced by the equity account of the social fund, so the value of the social assets would not determine the issuing value of the stock. The stock could be issued—as with a new company—for an arbitrarily set cash price. Each of the smaller divisional firms might own a part of the new apex company in proportion to the number of workers in the divisional firm. Some

of the shares in the apex firm might be retained as worker shares for the people who remain in the original firm.

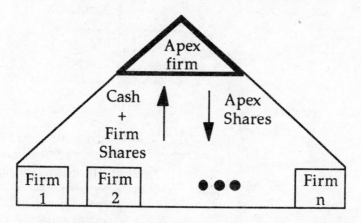

Figure 8.4 Separate Worker-owned Divisional Firms

(4) The separate divisional firms and the remaining parent firm join together in a federation with the parent firm as the apex organization performing appropriate functions such as strategic planning, marketing for the group, import-export for the group, and settling conflicts between the divisional firms. The money paid back to the apex firm would allow it to also act as a development bank for the group.

(5) Then each of the divisional firms buys in an ESOP-type credit transaction the assets it needs for its operations from the apex firm. The apex firm might also obtain some of the preferred (profit-sharing) or common shares in the divisional firms in exchange for the assets. In the divisional firms, the assets would no longer be social assets. Instead the money paid back to the parent firm would be social property.

(6) The operations of the divisions is switched over to the separate democratic worker-owned companies.

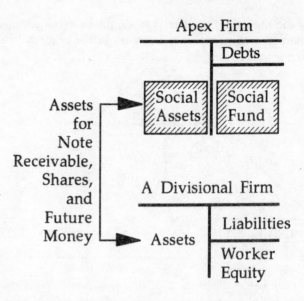

Figure 8.5 Divisional Firm Buying Assets with Credit and Shares

If the parent firm is not to be broken up into smaller units then a simpler model of restructuring might be used. Create a new social enterprise and transfer both the social assets and the social liability (or social fund) to the new enterprise. The original company converts into a worker-owned company that buys or leases back the assets. The social property is again separated away from the operating company (to minimize future political interference) and there is no need to rewrite the contracts of the existing company. The firm would always have the option of later dividing into smaller units.

The Chinese Enterprise Reforms

Introduction

The massacre of students and workers in Tiananmen Square and elsewhere in Beijing in June of 1989 has cast a pall over Chinese economic reforms. The speed and indeed the direction of further reforms will not be determined until after the power struggles that are sure to follow Deng Xiaoping's eventual death. We cannot pretend to know the outcome. Hence we can now only describe the reforms that led up to June 1989.

Agricultural Reforms

Deng Xiaoping is the godfather of the Chinese agricultural reforms. Although Deng is sometimes credited with initiating the reforms, it may be more accurate to describe him as giving official recognition and guidance to a popular trend in the countryside that began without Beijing's blessing.

The communes or collective farms were broken up into family-sized units who leased the land from the local government in the "family contract responsibility system."

The success in the countryside laid the foundation for Deng's power and for that of his one-time protégé, Zhao Ziyang. That success has given the Chinese the political leeway to extend the reforms to the state socialist organization of industry. In contrast, Gorbachev started with industrial restructuring. In spite of Gorbachev rising to power as an agricultural expert and in spite of the Chinese precedent, it took him four years before a similar agricultural leasing program was inaugurated in the Soviet Union early in 1989.

Lessons From Agriculture for Industry?

What are the lessons of the Chinese agricultural reform program for their industrial enterprise reforms? The family farm on long-term leased land is a compromise that happily avoids the difficult questions involved in industrial enterprises.

To own a physical asset is to own the stream of services provided by the asset plus the scrap left at the end of its economic lifetime. If the asset has indefinite economic lifetime (like most land), then an indefinite lease on the physical asset is the economic equivalent of ownership (except for marketability). In the Chinese family contract responsibility system, the lease is physical rather than financial, but it is long-term and stable so it is very close to the "ownership" the family would have if it borrowed the money and bought the land. With a long-term lease contract and a stable membership in the leasee group (e.g. the family), there is an economic incentive to plow back earnings to maintain and improve the asset.

An industrial enterprise is significantly different. The physical assets that are plant and equipment have a much shorter economic lifetime; they can be obsolete in five to ten years. Investment in an industrial firm is not an occasional matter (like building an irrigation system); it is a continuous process that is very much a part of the business. A physical lease is rather unwieldy in that context. One can imagine the bargaining between a lease enterprise and the ministry as to who will pay to modernize a line of machinery, install a new power system, build a new wing on the building, and so forth. A financial lease would be more practical.

It should be carefully noted that this argument for a financial lease or loan to buy depreciable industrial assets does not apply to the land itself. One could well have a worker-owned enterprise that borrowed the funds to buy ownership of the buildings and equipment—but that operated on land leased from the government (say, with a fifty year lease). In general, the more maintenance and replacement reinvestment required by an asset, the stronger is the argument for the user owning the asset rather than leasing it.

Moreover, beyond the level of the family shop, the members of the industrial enterprise are typically unrelated by family ties. It cannot be assumed that the members will automatically want their reinvested profits to be donated as "patrimony" to the next generation of members. When profits are reinvested to buy new assets, an internal capital account system would keep track of the part of the asset value that had not been depreciated or cancelled by other losses when a worker leaves so the worker would eventually receive back that "unused" value. If the retiring worker had a son or daughter coming to work in the enterprise, then the remaining account balance could be rolled over into a son or daughter's account as patrimony. But a retiring worker would also have the choice of having the account paid out. None of these questions arose in the case of a simple agricultural lease to a stable family unit.

The family farm operating on leased land is a non-threatening compromise because it does not force a separation between the two socialist traditions: state-socialism and self-managed socialism. The means of production, i.e. the land, are publicly owned so it satisfies that fetish of state-socialism. The family farm operating without hired labor is a small self-managed firm so it qualifies as an example of self-managed socialism. The "contradiction" between the two socialist traditions will become more acute in the industrial reforms.

The Factory Manager Responsibility System

The first attempt to extend the agricultural reforms into industry was based on a poor set of analogies. The manager rather than the workforce in the firm was taken as the party to the contract, and the contract was not a lease of the means of production. The purpose of the manager responsibility system was to transfer more decentralized control to the managers in state-owned firms. Moreover, the firms are supposed to be financially autonomous. The government has even used the expression "separation of ownership and control" as if that were a desirable feature of the American corporate world to be imitated.

The results of the manager responsibility system have been rather ambiguous. The system does not change residual claimancy. The workers in the state enterprises are still government employees. The manager and the workers have no definite property rights in the enterprise. The enterprise is still "owned" by the state and would be rescued by the government if it ran into trouble. The manager responsibility system is similar to the system used in the Hungarian New Economic Mechanism or NEM that has borne only limited fruit.

Experiments have taken place with a number of real changes in ownership structure. One experiment is to lease the physical means of production either to the workforce of the enterprise or to a private individual who hires the workers. We will later discuss physical leases to the workers in the context of *perestroika* in the Soviet Union where that experiment seems more widespread than in China.

The leasing to private individuals in China is at least of some importance in that it raises basic ideological questions about socialism. The two socialisms of state-socialism and self-management socialism have "two capitalisms" as their mirror reflections. State socialism sees "capitalism" as being based on *private* ownership of the means of production, while self-management socialism sees "capitalism" as being based on wage labor, the employer–employee relationship.

The "What is Capitalism?" debate—which is the mirror image of the "What is Socialism?" debate—is starting to emerge in China.

> Socialism as a body of anti-capitalist critiques and of systemic ideals has two related but distinct tenets or themes that appeal to different people—the *anti-market-anarchy* tenet that postulates state planning and control of the economy to the delight of political leaders and state bureaucrats, and the *anti-capitalist-exploiters* tenet that promises industrial democracy and workers' self-management ("masters of the means of production"). (Hsu, 1988, p. 1226)

When a government-owned factory is leased to an individual to operate with hired labor, that model is clearly rejected by self-management socialism and it makes only a fetishistic bow towards state socialism since the government still owns the means of production. Some officials have nevertheless claimed that such enterprises are still "socialist" even though the state is no longer the residual claimant and only has the role of rent collector. Others drawing on the *"anti-capitalist-exploiters* tenet" have claimed that the leasee individuals are only "capitalists without capital" (Deliusin, 1988, p. 1108), i.e. employers of hired labor operating with leased capital.

In another experiment widely reported in the West, state firms are restructured as corporations with salable securities and then a small portion of "stock" is sold to the workers and in some cases to outsiders. Although called "stock," the securities are more like variable income bonds. Early in 1989, experiments of selling stock to outsiders were discouraged.

Hundreds of state enterprises have set up *ad hoc* minority stock ownership programs for their workers. For instance, the Shenyang Alloy Plant is a state enterprise with 1100 workers that has instituted an innovative worker stock program. The honorary chairman of the board is Jiang Yiwei, editor of the journal, *Reform*, the intellectual leader of the economic democracy school which promotes worker ownership and self-management socialism as a model for reforms on the national level (see Jiang, 1988).

The Collective Sector

The Chinese economy can be divided into three sectors, the state sector ("ownership by all the people"), the collective sector ("ownership by the collectivity of workers in the firm"), and the private sector (e.g. micro-enterprises run by individuals). The existence of the collective sector is already a large step towards self-management socialism. Both state ownership and collective ownership are accepted as "socialist ownership forms." "Collectives" in China do not have any of the counter-cultural connotation they have in the USA or the UK. Most of the light industrial plants that have sprung up around the cities—often with people no longer needed in agriculture—have been organized as collectives. There are about 60 million workers in rural collectives and 40 million in urban collectives so, in total, the workforce in collectives is comparable to the entire American workforce.

In reality, the collectives are usually far from being worker self-managed. They are usually run by some combination of the city, country, township, or village governments. Since they are already nominally owned by the collectivity of workers, the collectives have been the most active and creative in setting up worker stock programs. Hundreds and perhaps thousands of collectives across China have inaugurated *ad hoc* worker ownership programs.

The northern city of Shenyang (which used to be Mukden) has been a leader in the worker stock experiments in collectives as well as in state enterprises. The worker stock is a kind of profit-sharing certificate which can pay from 3 per cent to 20 per cent of face value per year as a dividend. The workers may also through their stockholders' assembly elect the board and perhaps even the manager.

In the summer of 1988, the author visited a number of worker stock experiments as the guest of Luo Xiaopeng of the Research Center for Rural Development. The Shenyang Small

Compressor Factory was particularly interesting. It was previously a city-run collective that is now called a "stock cooperative." It makes small air compressors and has 830 workers. The workers elect both the board and the manager. There is a nomination procedure for managers. The managers then have campaigns and finally there is a secret ballot election on a one-worker/one-vote basis. It is a presidential system with a directly elected manager as opposed to the usual parliamentary system used in Western companies where the board of directors (as the workplace parliament) selects the manager. When asked what happened if the separately elected board disagreed with the manager on an important issue, the Chairman of the Board, who is the local Communist Party head, exclaimed "checks and balances"! They have also instituted a range of worker education and participation programs in the small compressor plant. According to the city officials, there are now about 300 enterprises in the Shenyang area using what they called "the small compressor model" named after that factory.

Interest in worker ownership has developed in China on a number of fronts. During the war against the Japanese and the Chinese Civil War, thousands of Gung Ho ("Working Together") worker cooperatives sprung up. After the Revolution, the Gung Ho cooperatives dwindled as an independent movement. With the recent reforms, that Gung Ho Cooperative Movement has started to revive itself. But the future of democratic worker ownership in China will be decided not by cooperative startups, but by the coming struggles for power in the political arena.

9
Reforms in the USSR, Hungary, and Poland

Soviet Union: Gorbachev's *Perestroika*

The Revival of Worker Cooperatives

Perestroika is a multi-faceted process, but our focus is only on the role of worker ownership in the Soviet enterprise reforms. Worker ownership has so far appeared in three forms, worker cooperative startups, lease firms, and new ESOP-type worker buyouts.

There have always been "cooperatives" in Soviet-type economies but they were run by some level of government and were "cooperative" in name only. Thus the recent revival refers to worker cooperatives that are more genuine in the sense of not being part of the government apparatus (although they may also be just family-owned companies).

The ideological support for the revival goes back to Lenin. In 1923 and shortly before his death, Lenin dictated the work, *On Cooperatives*, which is now described as Lenin's last will and testament to socialism that was betrayed by Stalin. In a speech on March 23, 1988, Gorbachev noted that "as a result of departing from the Leninist principles of the cooperative movement, the country and its economy have suffered substantial setbacks in political, moral and social terms." He urged that the "cooperative movement ... be revived in all its diversity."

Worker cooperatives have in recent years been encouraged particularly in consumer services (e.g. restaurants, medical services, barbers, hairdressers, and so forth), consumer goods, and light industry. Over 100,000 cooperatives have sprung up in recent years—although many may be family operations called "cooperatives" for ideological protection.

The ministries charge cooperatives up to six times as much as other state firms for some inputs in the state sector (Nuti, 1988b, p. 13). The co-ops have nevertheless been so successful that a backlash has already developed. The higher quality of goods and services available from the cooperatives and the higher costs result in long lines (one rationing mechanism) and then in higher prices (another rationing mechanism). The real or imagined higher incomes of the co-op members triggered the *ressentiment* that lurks beneath the surface of "socialist equality." In the recent Siberian miners' strikes, one of the demands, little reported in the Western press, was to shut down a number of cooperatives. Instead of encouraging more cooperatives so that competition would drive down prices, bureaucrats, who had their own reasons for resenting independent economic activity, responded with a number of regulations on the prices and activities of cooperatives.

There are stories across the Soviet Union of worker cooperatives battling entrenched bureaucracies. Near Minsk, about 800 workers were employed in an electrical insulation factory. The factory didn't want to produce some needed consumer goods that were not in the plan so four workers asked to start up a cooperative to produce the goods. Within one year, 700 workers had left the factory to work in the cooperative where they could get 800 roubles a month in comparison with the previous average of 200 roubles a month. The manager protested "I created you—don't take my workers," turned off the electricity, and took away the crane the workers had been using. After some negotiation, the cooperative finally started producing again. Then the manager announced that he wanted to join the cooperative—but the Ministry said that was enough. They formed an "association" with the cooperative that raked off most of the income of the cooperative as a "rent" for the use of state assets.

As cooperatives further develop, they will probably have their greatest effect in consumer goods and services. They will take some pressure off the state sector, but it is questionable how far they will penetrate into the state sector. The cooperative form has been used more to start new businesses than to convert state-owned firms into worker-owned firms.

Leasing in Industry and Agriculture

A number of state-run firms have been converted to worker-run "lease firms." The leasing idea seems to have a genesis independent of the historical cooperative movement, and it is the industrial analogue of the leasing of agricultural land to families.

In a worker-owned firm, the traditional hiring relationship between capital and labor is reversed; labor hires capital. To transform a state-run enterprise into a worker-run enterprise, the hiring contract between the state and the workers would be reversed. Instead of the state hiring the workers, the workers of the enterprise would, in effect, hire or lease the capital from the state. That is the transformation in the state/workers' relationship described in abstract and simple terms.

There are many different ways to conceptually approach the idea and the reality of the worker-owned firm. The "leasing of capital" idea seems to be an approach gaining strength with *perestroika*. The idea of the worker-owned firm is approached as a group of workers collectively contracting to lease the necessary fixed assets, buy the inputs, and sell their output.

Prominent supporters of leasing include Academician Abel Aganbegyan, one of Gorbachev's economic advisors on *perestroika*, Academician Leonid Abalkin, a new deputy prime minister, Oleg Bogomolov, Director of the Institute of Economics of World Socialist Systems, and Academician Tatiana Zaslavskaya, a sociologist and chief pollster in Gorbachev's kitchen cabinet (see Schroeder, 1988). Dr Valery Rutgaizer, deputy director of Zaslavskaya's All-Union Center for Public Opinion Research, is one of the leading practitioners and promoters of the leasing firms.

The political justification for leasing goes back to Lenin's New Economic Policy or NEP started in 1921. Instead of arbitrary requisitions of grain from the peasants, the peasants paid a fixed rent or tax, and then kept the remainder to use or sell. Some factories were even leased back to their previous owners in order to restart industry after the ravages of the 1917 Revolution and the Civil War. Lenin died in 1924 and by the end of the decade, Stalin had turned the country towards collectivisation in agriculture and state-socialism in industry.

In the 1960s, contract collectives were used in agricultural production by I. Khudenko in Kazakhstan. In a specialized plant-growing collective, productivity was seven to nine times the regional average "exceeding even American levels." These results pointed to the misuse of resources elsewhere. Public officials persecuted Khudenko using trumped-up charges. Aganbegyan and Zaslavskaya, then in Novosibirsk, wrote letters to support Khudenko but to no avail [see Aganbegyan, 1988]. He died in jail.

A form of team incentive contract was used successfully during the 1970s by the lawyer, agronomist, and First Secretary of the Stavropol region, Mikhail Gorbachev.

> In effect, the reform Gorbachev adopted allowed a handful of farm workers to sign a contract with their collective under which they would take on responsibility for a patch of land. They would plough, sow, weed, fertilise it, and supervise the harvest. They would be paid by results—a strong incentive—and they would be responsible for the same patch of land each year, which gave them a further incentive to treat and prepare the land well, rather than exhaust it, and to supervise drainage throughout the winter. (Walker, 1988, p. 16)

The results, a 20–30 per cent increase in productivity, helped propel Gorbachev to national attention.

In 1978, Gorbachev became the Central Committee's Secretary of Agriculture in Moscow. When Brezhnev died, his successor, Andropov, promised "a wider independence and autonomy for industrial associations and farms." Gorbachev announced the

> "collective contract in farm production": giving autonomous teams of farm workers the right to draw up long-term contracts with management that would let them organize their own work, and decide their own pay packets, which would be linked to the amount of food they produced. Moreover, Gorbachev added, these teams

166

should be allowed to elect their own leaders. (Walker, 1988, pp. 19–20)

The results were rather mixed since the idea met resistance at many levels, particularly from the management of the collective farm.

It should be carefully noted that these autonomous work teams are not leasing arrangements—although they are a step in that direction. The team contracts are essentially a form of collective piece-rate work. A piece-rate worker differs from a true independent producer of a product. The independent producer pays for his inputs and owns the outputs; the piece-rate worker does neither. Similarly, a true leasing collective would pay for its inputs and sell its outputs; the autonomous teams neither paid for their inputs nor owned their outputs. They were simply paid a collective piece-rate according to their results.

After Gorbachev rose to power in 1984, he moved in a few years from the collective piece-rate teams to support of leasing collectives. Even in the collective piece-rate arrangement, the worker is still an employee or hired laborer for the collective farm or state farm—and that is the root of the problem.

What is the problem here? Comrades, the main thing now is the fact that the economic relations that have developed in the countryside today clearly do not provide people with an incentive to creative, active, enterprising labor. What has happened is that on collective farms and state farms man has been torn away from the land, from the means of production. ... A person comes to a farm as a hired laborer, in order to put in a certain number of hours doing something or other; after all, he has to earn a living. (Gorbachev, *Pravda*, Oct. 14, 1988, translated in Gorbachev, 1988b, p. 2)

Citing Lenin's NEP- as a precedent, Gorbachev calls for leasing as a way to "return people to the land as full-fledged masters." Moreover, Gorbachev notes how the lease contract differs from the previous collective piece-rate contract.

The [collective] contract is a major step, and a lease is also a type of contract, but its highest form—the lease contract, in which a person leases both land and means of production for a certain period of time and is linked only by economic relations to the farm from which he received the land—this is something totally different.
...Through lease contracts and lease relations, a colossal democratization is taking place not only of the economy but also of society as a whole.... This is an extremely thoroughgoing, revolutionary restructuring. (Gorbachev, 1988b, pp. 4–6)

In mid-March 1989, Gorbachev announced a sweeping new law finally giving a statutory basis for agricultural leasing. Families can lease land for a lifetime and then the lease can be inherited. With that policy, Gorbachev is at last following Deng Xiaoping's successful agricultural reform based on long-term leasing of the land from the commune to farm families in the contract responsibility system.

Lease Firms

According to Dr Valery Rutgaizer, there are over 1000 industrial enterprises in the Moscow area using the leasing system. The gross in these enterprises is up an average of 25 per cent. Service companies have improved efficiency with 15 per cent less workers. When polled, 60 per cent of managers found they had real economic independence.

The lease is a contract between the new enterprise as a legal entity and the owner of the assets. The lease enterprises are structured as *ad hoc* collectives—creatures of the lease contract.

Some of the workers fear the leasing system. It may expose redundancy and it gives them no wage guarantee. Moreover, they think that the lease firms require more intense labor. Dr Rutgaizer emphasized that the very success of the leasing co-ops would endanger them unless there was also changes in the government bureaucracy. He cited examples such as the lease of some taxicabs to drivers. Their income shot up to 700 roubles a month (average factory wage is around 200 roubles), and the experiment was discontinued.

The State Enterprise Restructuring Law of 1987

The leasing system is not (yet) the centerpiece of the industrial restructuring program. The current program is outlined in the State Enterprise Law of 1987 and is to be fully implemented by 1990. These proposed enterprise reforms are "weak beer" compared to the autonomy and self-responsibility of the lease firms and cooperatives. The "weak beer" reforms are similar to the Hungarian New Economic Mechanism (NEM) of 1968 that met with rather limited success and that now needs to be extended to "ownership" questions [see below]. The enterprises remain state firms and the workers remain state employees. But the enterprises will have more financial autonomy and more freedom from Gosplan directives. After certain charges (taxes or rents) are remitted to the government, the enterprise can keep the remainder. Most of the retained income must be reinvested but a certain portion can be distributed as a profit-sharing bonus to the workers. There may even be some election of managers by the workers.

The results so far have not been encouraging.

> One giant stride was meant to be the move of the entire economy at the beginning of this year to "self-financing". This is turning out to be an embarrassed shuffle. Some two-thirds of factories had already moved last year to supposedly greater independence under the Law on the State Enterprise, which was heralded as the cornerstone of the economic reforms. The disastrous result was to discredit the reforms before they had got fully under way. (*The Economist*, January 14, 1989, pp. 44–5)

In spite of the profit-sharing and increased autonomy, this Russian version of NEM reforms will *not* give the workers a sense of "ownership"; it is only a half-way house.

The Importance of Leasing

In the same issue of *The Economist* containing Dr Rutgaizer's report on leasing, there is an article on *perestroika* ("Every step hurts") which cites a vision of the future Soviet economy due to the radical reformer economist, Nikolai Shmelev.

> Peer into the future, and the Soviet economy may look something like this. About 30% of it will be private-sector, but called co-operative-sector out of ideological propriety. The state will have loosened its grip on the remaining 70%, through some sort of share-issuing and through collective leasing.... (*The Economist*, January 14, 1989, p. 44)

The key role of leasing in this scenario indicates its importance as a means to move away from the state operation of large enterprises.

The leasing system is important because it provides a means to move from the NEM-type reforms of the 1987 Enterprise Law (increased autonomy and financial accountability of state firms) to a change in "ownership" (labor hiring or leasing capital and taking on the residual claimant role).

Gorbachev's remarks about the agricultural leasing system making the farmer into the master of the land and means of production has a natural extension to the industrial leasing system and the industrial workers. Gorbachev's support for the leasing system should strengthen and accelerate the development of lease firms reported by Dr Rutgaizer.

There are questions of socialist ideology involved with cooperatives or lease firms. A genuine cooperative or lease firm is not owned or operated by the government. The workers in the cooperative are the residual claimants and control the production process. State socialism focuses on state ownership so a worker co-op would not be "socialist." However, self-management socialism emphasizes replacing wage-labor (with a private or public employer) with "free associations of producers." Clearly worker co-ops and lease firms represent a move away from hired labor in the direction of that non-governmental form of socialism based on free associations of producers (see Kushnirsky, 1987 on a worker ownership model for the *perestroika*).

Physical and Financial Leasing

"Ownership of the firm" is a phrase that often refers to two conceptually distinct roles: (a) ownership of the means of production in the sense of plant, equipment, and other material inputs, and (b) being the residual claimant, namely the legal party who bears the costs of production (including lease payments and costs of other inputs) and owns the product. Physical leasing changes the residual claimant without changing the ownership of the physical assets used in production, i.e. without changing the "ownership of the means of production." The residual claimant has the use rights over the assets without the ownership rights.

For workers to be the residual claimants, they must rent or lease the capital they use, i.e. labor must hire the capital. But there are two different ways to hire capital:

(1) to physically lease capital goods (machines, buildings, and land), or
(2) to borrow financial capital which can then be used to buy the physical capital goods.

With either the physical lease or the financial lease (loan), labor hires capital and the workers as a legal body are the residual claimant.

The two lease methods however have different dynamic and psychological aspects. The physical lease system is quite clumsy in many ways. Consider maintenance. An outside owner of the physical assets would hardly have the appropriate information for efficient maintenance. Yet if the workers were responsible for maintenance, then they would be maintaining physical assets they do not own so one would not expect the maintenance work to be of high caliber (compare how a person maintains a rental car versus his own car purchased with borrowed money).

Consider capital improvements and new replacement or net investment. It would be incredibly unwieldy if the workers had to get the government to make all the investments they need in physical assets so the workers could then again lease what they need. And if the workers' enterprise reinvested its own earnings on new physical assets, who would own the new assets? If the new assets were owned by the enterprise, then the system would slowly change over to using enterprise-owned physical assets (as the government assets are depreciated and replaced). If the new assets were government-owned, that would sharply reduce the incentive for reinvestment by the enterprise. Why not avoid the inefficiencies and complications of the physical leases of *depreciable* assets by using financial leases in the first place?

These arguments do not apply to non-depreciable assets such as land. The workers' enterprise could borrow the financial capital (take out a financial lease) to purchase the depreciable assets of the old enterprise while taking out a long-term physical lease on the land.

It would be unfortunate if the government resisted a financial lease arrangement (which would allow the workers' enterprise to purchase the depreciable assets) because of the old slogans about "state ownership of the means of production." The important part of "ownership of the firm" is the residual claimancy, and that has *already* switched to the workers' hands with the physical lease. "Refinancing" the physical lease of the depreciable assets with a financial lease would only make the whole arrangement more rational and efficient from the viewpoint of capital maintenance and reinvestment.

Using ESOP-type Financial Lease Transactions

In the West, almost all worker-owned companies are, for the above reasons, based on financial leases rather than physical leases. Labor hires financial capital, not physical capital.

In a state-socialist country, the transition to worker-owned firms would amount to a reversal of the hiring contract between the state and the workers. Instead of state-owned capital hiring the workers, the workers through their legal embodiment in the enterprise would hire the capital (financial or physical) from the state. In a given enterprise, this contract reversal could occur all at once—going from 100 per cent state-residual-claimancy to 100 per cent worker-residual-claimancy, *or* it could be developed slowly over a period of years with the intermediate enterprise being partly state and partly worker residual claimancy.

In either case, the enterprise needs to be legally organized as a legal company separate from the government. That company structure should embody share capital accounts for each worker (even if the accounts start off with little or no capital). If there was to be a gradual transition to worker ownership, then the company would start off being wholly-owned by the government. There are several ways to structure the transition. One way to start the transition is to simply endow the workers with a certain percentage of the ownership in recognition of their past labor. That initial endowment could be split among the capital accounts in proportion to their seniority and pay level within the enterprise.

The American ESOP is a special loan or financial lease arrangement used to *increase* the proportion of worker equity in the company.

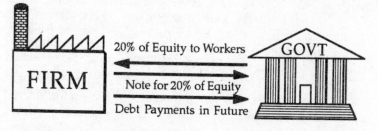

Figure 9.1   Example of ESOP-type Financial Lease Transaction

Suppose the workers already have 40 per cent of the equity and are going to add on another 20 per cent so they become 60 per cent equityholders in the company. The equity of the company is currently divided 40 per cent workers and 60 per cent state. Then the worker portion of the equity (functioning as an "internal ESOP") takes out a loan from the government equal to 20 per cent of the equity and uses the proceeds to buy that 20 per cent of the equity from the self-same government. In sum, this paper transaction gives the government a debt note in exchange for transferring 20 per cent of the equity over to the workers' accounts. The note is then paid off over a period of years. The transaction might also be lubricated with special tax breaks (but that is less relevant in the socialist context when the state is the banker, the retiring owner, and the tax collector).

The New ESOP-type Worker Buyouts in the USSR

This book must now become self-referential. The first draft of this book was given in January 1989 to Dr Rutgaizer at the Oxford Conference on Industrial Partnerships and Worker-owned Businesses sponsored by Robert Oakeshott of Job Ownership Ltd of London and co-sponsored by the Industrial Cooperative Association. The manuscript contained the model for the hybrid democratic firm and the argument given above for moving beyond the physical lease to a financial lease—for moving from a worker leaseout to a worker buyout of state sector firms. Robert Oakeshott and the author then visited Dr Rutgaizer in Moscow in June 1989 after a tour of worker-owned and self-managed firms in Poland and Hungary. The surprise was that Dr Rutgaizer had developed the model outlined in the manuscript for the particular Russian circumstances, and had thus created the first ESOP-type worker buyouts from the state sector in the Soviet Union (see *The Economist*, "Nothing to Lease but your chains," September 16, 1989, p. 51).

The first worker buyouts of state-owned firms were arranged in a Moscow firm manufacturing food processing equipment and in a building materials firm outside Moscow. Both of the firms have operated for over a year as lease firms. The lease firm changes the profit claimant from the state to the workers' collective of the firm, but the state continues to have the ideologically important role of "owning the means of production." The worker buyouts go the next step of transferring the ownership of the means of production (the capital goods used by the firm) to the workers' firm in a credit transaction with the selling ministry supplying the credit.

Since a worker buyout of a state-owned firm is unprecedented in the modern Soviet Union, it must be approved by the Council of Deputies' Standing Commission on Economic Reform headed by the leading *perestroika* economist, Academician Leonid Abalkin—who is solidly behind the worker buyouts.

The Soviet Union has nothing resembling Anglo-American trust law so the ESOP has to be "internal" to the company instead of as a separate trust. This, however, only makes a necessity out of a virtue since the whole ESOP structure can be much simplified and streamlined by making it part of the company itself. These first two Soviet "ESOPs" will have a local institution as the minority partner that may be later bought out.

The Soviet Union also does not have any useable private joint stock company law. This means that the lease firms are creatures of the lease contracts, and the worker-buyout ESOPs are, at least for now, creatures of their by-laws. The lease firms and the new ESOP-type firms are evolving as legal forms for companies separate from the cooperative form. Dr Rutgaizer is writing a first draft of proposed legislation for the lease firms and the ESOP-type firms.

The two ESOPs are democratic in the sense that the workers vote on a one-person/one-vote basis to elect the workers' council (or Board of Directors) and on all other votes put to the membership. Dr Rutgaizer calls this ESOP-like trust form of ownership *"kollektivnaya sobstvennost"* which he translates as "collective job ownership." "Collective" refers to the fact that—as in the American ESOP—the workers do not individually own shares that they can sell; the ownership is held in trust. However, there are individual capital accounts which record each worker-member's share of the net asset value.

The company manufacturing food processing equipment is called "Moscow Experimental Plant (Catering)" (a name it acquired in 1965 as a part of other experiments). It has about 700 workers. The company was originally set up in 1929 so a good part of the plant is 60 years old. The company was in a crisis several years ago when Gorbachev's anti-alcohol campaign sent the orders for bottling equipment plummeting. They were merged into a larger firm under a new supervisory ministry. A year ago, they became a separate firm again under another ministry. Tired of being merged and divided, they opted to become a lease firm.

When Dr Rutgaizer returned from Oxford in January, he published an article in *Isvestia* describing worker ownership in

America and the UK. The director of the food equipment company, Valery Gorokhov, (who in his thirties is one of the youngest plant directors in the Soviet Union) read the article and contacted Dr Rutgaizer to volunteer for the conversion from a lease firm to a worker-owned firm. They worked out the detailed by-laws, prepared the financial projections, and got the necessary approval from the Workers' Assembly by the middle of June. The minority partner will be a regional council, a unit of local government.

The construction materials plant is called the "Khljupin Building Materials Plant" (near Pushkin's home outside Moscow). It has about 650 workers. The company began in 1960 using outdated equipment from other plants. First, it make bricks, and then in 1970 it switched over to linoleum, vinyl wall-covering, and "poly-fillers" used in construction. The director, Boris Makharnov, has made the business profitable and is involved entrepreneurially in some joint ventures. He led the fight to become one of the first leasing firms—a particularly difficult fight since the ministry didn't want to give up a profitable firm. When describing the final leasing approval from the ministry, Dr Rutgaizer said "'Free at last' as on Martin Luther King's grave." The next step of the ESOP-style worker buyout is now being prepared [Fall 1989]. The likely minority partner in the buyout is one of their banks, the regional department of the Bank for Housing and Social Development.

These interesting and hopeful developments need to be placed in perspective. They are dwarfed by the enormous obstacles facing *perestroika* in the Soviet Union. How can the Communist Party fundamentally change the Party-controlled economy and still retain its "expected" role in society? In Eastern Europe (and the Baltic nations), a non-communist society is within living memory, and economic liberalization is fueled by the desire for national autonomy. But in Russia, state socialism has soaked into their bones on a surprisingly large scale, and the system was not imposed from the outside. It is an unoriginal but accurate observation that the best hope for the *perestroika* is that there is no other choice.

Hungary: A Socialist Wall Street?

Introduction: The NEM Reforms

With the exception of Yugoslavia, the Hungarian NEM (New Economic Mechanism) reforms, initiated in 1968, are the oldest in the socialist countries. Many of the recent reforms in other socialist countries (e.g. the 1987 Enterprise Law in the Soviet Union and manager responsibility system in China) which emphasize financial autonomy within a framework of state ownership are similar to the Hungarian NEM and will likely face the same difficulties in due time.

The basic idea of the NEM reforms was decentralized financially autonomous state firms operating in a partial market environment within a framework of state regulation. The Golden Age of the reforms was the period from 1968 to 1971 which was followed by a period of backsliding and some recentralization from 1972 to 1978. From 1979 to the present, the NEM has muddled along and been deepened in various ways. Debate rages in Hungary about the next steps—with some focus on the development of "full" capital markets.

To over-simplify, reformers may be divided into two camps: (1) the middle-of-the-road reformers who are basically content with muddling through within the current institutional framework of the NEM, and (2) the radical reformers who argue that the reforms can only be successful if totalized and completed by moving further in the direction of a market economy—particularly with the introduction of active credit and capital markets.

One group of radical reformers is associated with Márton Tardos, previously of the Institute for Financial Research. In the ups and downs of government policy, the Institute was abolished and some of the staff started a joint stock consultancy, Financial Research Ltd. The Tardos group has been particularly concerned with integrating public capital markets in some suitable form into the economic reform program (see Tardos, 1988). On the political side, the radical reformers are associated with the democratic reform leader and Politburo

177

member, Imre Pozsgay (see *The Economist*, March 18, 1989, pp. 44–6).

There is also a school of radical philosophy, the Budapest School, that strongly supports workers' self-management (see Brown, 1988).

Analysis and Criticism of the NEM

The Hungarian reforms starting in 1968 have been successful in several areas. The agricultural cooperative sector is probably the most genuine (i.e. not state-run) in Eastern Europe and it has been quite productive. Small family-run private businesses have been allowed to flourish (a very recent development in the Soviet Union) in the "second economy." There are not only markets in consumer goods but also in capital goods and productive inputs. Enterprises are allowed to issue bonds which can be purchased by other enterprises or individuals—so a bond market has developed.

The heart of the reforms in the state enterprise sector has been less successful. There is no firm line between state and enterprise; the state regulators can still intervene in hundreds of ways to compromise enterprise autonomy. True autonomy implies full "up-side potential" and "down-side risk," while the Hungarian state firms have both their incentives and risks softened by state regulation. If the enterprise does very well then, as with the piece-worker, the "norm" will be ratcheted up. In this case, the taxes and other charges levied on the enterprises will rise to weaken their profit incentive. On the downside, the government provides a "soft budget constraint." Distressed firms are subsidized and reorganized so that bankruptcy is not a credible threat.

In the 1980s, the reforms have progressed by increasing worker influence through the election of managers. But if the workers have no capital accounts in the enterprise, then this will lead to the distortions of the Yugoslav self-management system. The workers will only receive value from the enterprise in one pocket, namely wages and bonuses. They will tend to elect managers to maximize the short-term payout and that will, in turn, lead to more *ad hoc* bureaucratic interference in

178

the Yugoslav manner to preserve and increase the long-term capital value of the enterprise.

Worker self-management should be completed with share capital accounts giving workers the "other pocket" representing the net asset value of the enterprise. Then the decision to pay out profits from the enterprise is the decision to take value out of one pocket (the workers' capital interest in the enterprise) and put it in their other pocket (wages and bonuses)—which may or may not be a good idea depending on the relative opportunities of the two uses of the profits.

In brief, the NEM reforms were not very successful because they gave the enterprises only (weak) financial autonomy rather than true ownership autonomy. As they now stand, the state firms have ownership-by-everybody which functions as ownership-by-nobody. Only firms with clear ownership autonomy can reap the efficiency of a decentralized market economy. And if the autonomous ownership is *worker* ownership, then the firms can also reap the X-efficiency of heightened worker motivation and effort.

Paths to Worker Ownership

The path of reforms in the socialist countries is an ever-narrowing spiral revolving around the central issue of *ownership* of the firm (particularly "ownership" in the sense of residual claimancy). Sooner or later, socialist reforms will be drawn into the heart of the "ownership question." As long as government ownership remains the *sanctum sanctorum* of socialist ideology, there will be no solution.

Professor János Kornai, who is sympathetic to but not now an active member of the radical reformers, has noted that the "problem of ownership and property rights is not clearly elaborated in the writings of the radical reformers." (Kornai, 1986, p. 1733) Worker ownership is unfortunately best known in Eastern Europe by the Yugoslav example with its flawed capital rights structure. Labor-based worker-owned firms with share capital accounts as represented by the Mondragon worker cooperatives in Spain and the democratic ESOPs in America are less well-known in Eastern Europe.

179

One path to work ownership in Hungary is the worker cooperatives. There is a sizable sector of rather authentic worker cooperatives in Hungary, and they provide an example of non-government ownership that has always been recognized in socialist theory. There is also a relatively new legal form of the "small cooperative" that is used in the small business sector. But Hungarian cooperatives, like all socialist cooperatives in varying degrees, suffer from "social property" capital structures and excessive state interference. With proper organization and improved capital structures, the cooperative sector in Hungary should grow.

The leasing idea is another path that has been developed in Hungary. One of the pioneers of the radical reform movement, Tibor Liska, outlined schemes to lease out state capital in the 1960s (see Bárony, 1982; or *The Economist*, March 19, 1983). In the NEM reforms, a number of small shops and enterprises were leased out to their workers or even to private individuals hiring a few workers.

> This form [leasing] is widely applied in trade and in the restaurant sector. Fixed capital remains in state ownership, but the business is run by a private individual who pays a rent fixed by a contract and also taxes. He keeps the profit or covers the deficit at his own risk.... In 1984 about 11% of the shops and 37% of the restaurants were leased this way. (Kornai, 1986, p. 1709)

Hungary is moving away from the "monobank system" so that firms can eventually obtain credit from a variety of competing financial institutions. A bond market has also been developed, and a "stock market" and a mutual fund are scheduled to open. The ESOP loan transaction was previously described with the state acting as the source of credit. In Hungary, the other sources of capital and credit would facilitate the use of the ESOP-type transaction if the corporate form was available.

Individual worker-owned firms or consortia of such firms could also market risk-capital instruments such as participating debt securities, profit-sharing stock (non-voting preferred stock adapted to worker ownership) or variable income bonds. Thus the X-efficiency of worker-owned firms can be developed along with the risk allocative efficiency of public capital markets carrying financial instruments or securities with varying degrees of risk and reward [these questions will be addressed more in the next chapter].

Poland: Self-Management and Solidarity

Introduction

Poland's situation is somewhat unique due to Solidarity— which has functioned less as a trade union than as a national oppositional party. In its early days prior to the imposition of martial law, Solidarity intellectuals issued a manifesto calling for workers' self-management. The model was only out-lined and was roughly along Yugoslav lines in that it did not address the capital rights issue. In any case, that initiative was pushed into the background with the imposition of martial law in December 1981 and the outlawing of Solidarity.

The recent (prior to the Solidarity-led government) economic reform plan was similar to the Hungarian NEM in that it promoted financial autonomy in the state sector and promoted private/cooperative forms of enterprise for small businesses. Given the deteriorated state of the Polish economy, there was little hope that the program would have even the modest success of the 1968 Hungarian NEM reforms.

Today it is unclear to what extent workers' self-management is at the top of Solidarity's economic agenda. A worker owner-ship agenda would imply a willingness to take responsibility at the enterprise level, and that means moving well beyond the "traditional" union role.

The Self-Management Councils

The idea of workers' self-management based on enterprise workers' councils dates back to the postwar period in Poland; programs involving workers' councils were advanced in 1945, 1956, and 1981 (see Holland, 1988). During the 1980–1981 heyday of Solidarity, workers' councils were spontaneously elected in a number of enterprises. The Party even supported the effort in hope of outflanking Solidarity, but Solidarity responded by making self-management part of its program in the summer of 1981. Compromise legislation for workers' councils was passed in September 1981, but the active development was halted by martial law in December of 1981.

> Polish workers wanted greater participation in workplace decision-making, but like the Hungarians in 1956, they were beginning to struggle with the tough questions of property ownership. They rejected the principle of state ownership and control of the means of production, but simultaneously they did not want to turn their factories over to private individuals. It is possible that had the social movements consolidated by Solidarity not been crushed, they would have gravitated towards forms of ownership compatible with self-management. (Brown, 1988, p. 202)

In the post-martial-law period of the early 1980s, the government promoted workers' councils or self-management councils in the state firms to function as government and management-controlled transmission belts. But with the passage of time, some of the worker councils started to become more autonomous.

Just as the various reforms try to promote some enterprise autonomy from the state through the horizontal interaction of firms on the market, so the worker councils decided that horizontal association was their path to independence from the state. In the fall of 1985, 25 of the most independent worker councils convened in Torun but the government would not allow a meeting fearing another oppositional party. In reply, a group of "radical" activists called for the creation of a national workers' council alliance. But calmer heads prevailed on them to withdraw their proposal. Too many of the councils were then dominated by the government so any alliance open to all worker councils would not be independent of government influence.

Finally a compromise was reached to start an *Association of Self-Management Activists* (ASMA). In November 1987, 45 representatives of the biggest industrial enterprises endorsed the idea. The government considered it a threat to the status quo but, after negotiation, the group received permission to hold a founding meeting early in 1988.

At the same time, the group started to form alliances of the stronger worker councils on a regional basis. Alliances have now been formed in Warsaw, Gdansk, Torun, Opole, Poznan, and Wroclaw, with others being prepared. The ASMA group held at the end of 1988 a self-management forum for several regional alliances, and it has plans for a *Self-Management Institute* in 1989.

The ASMA group and the regional alliances of the worker councils are so new that one cannot judge the eventual import of this development. But they are surely "part of the solution," and will promote the future development of democratic worker-ownership in Poland. Through the work of Solidarity and the workers' councils, "the *idea* of self-management has become well established in the Polish working class" (Holland, 1988, p. 140).

The large Polish state-owned enterprises with strong worker councils seem ripe for the decentralizing model of privatization with worker ownership. The workers in a division can form a separate joint stock company which can then buy the requisite assets from the parent company. The assets would be purchased partly on a credit basis to be repaid in the future and partly in return for shares going to the parent company. In this manner, the parent company could repeatedly spin off majority worker-owned companies which would be joined together in a federation with the parent company as the apex company [see the previous discussion in the context of the Yugoslavian reforms].

10
Analysis of the Socialist Enterprise Reforms

Socialist Enterprise Reform Programs: Where Are They Going?

In most socialist countries today, there is a movement away from the state-socialist model of government ownership and centralized planning towards some more decentralized economy with markets playing a larger role. *Perestroika* in the Soviet Union and *gai-ge* in China have been much in the headlines. More attention is now being lavished on the reforms in Hungary and Poland as they are rapidly moving towards a decentralized system.

The Western press tends to interpret any movement away from state-socialism as a movement towards capitalism. There is, however, another interpretation. The socialist enterprise reforms could be interpreted as movements away from the socialism of the state towards the other socialist tradition of *self-management socialism*, the socialism of the workers which emphasized the "free association of producers" instead of state ownership of the means of production.

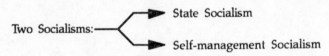

Two Socialisms: State Socialism / Self-management Socialism

Figure 10.1 The Two Socialisms

That self-management socialism is theoretically compatible with all markets except the market in labor and the market in equity shares in productive enterprises.

184

The "Two Socialisms" and the "Two Capitalisms"

"Ownership" is the issue—but what is "ownership of the firm"? In the West, the phrase "ownership of the firm" combines two rather different things:

(1) the *ownership of the capital goods* and other means of production, and
(2) the contractual role of being the *residual claimant* (the legal party who buys or already owns the inputs used up in production and who appropriates and sells the outputs).

What is the *sine qua non* of capitalist production:
— private ownership of capital goods, *or*
— non-labor residual claimancy (i.e. the residual claimant is the capitalist or someone other than the collectivity of workers in an enterprise)?

The two answers give "two capitalisms" which correlate with the two socialist traditions: state socialism and self-management socialism.

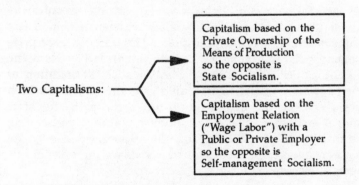

Two Capitalisms:

Capitalism based on the Private Ownership of the Means of Production so the opposite is State Socialism.

Capitalism based on the Employment Relation ("Wage Labor") with a Public or Private Employer so the opposite is Self-management Socialism.

Figure 10.2 The Two Capitalisms

State socialism identified capitalism with the *"private ownership of the means of production"* so "socialism" would have to be based on government ownership. A worker-owned firm would be seen as "worker capitalism" simply because it was not government owned—regardless of whether or not it had a democratic labor-based membership structure.

Self-management socialism would, in contrast, take capitalism as being based on the employment relation which allowed some legal party other than the collectivity of workers in the enterprise to be the residual claimant. Hence the state-owned firm would be criticized as a form of "state capitalism."

The enterprise reform programs in the socialist countries are now coming to the crucial junction, reforming "ownership." That brings to the foreground the rather deep-lying confusion in socialist countries over the *sine qua non* of capitalist production. As noted previously in China, there have been examples where local governments have leased the "means of production" to individuals who hire workers as employees, and then the officials claim that it is still "socialist" since the government retains ownership of the capital goods. These examples highlight the almost fetishistic importance of the "government ownership of the means of production" in the countries with a tradition of state socialism.

The transition from state-socialism to some form of self-management socialism is not new. For several decades, the Yugoslavian economy has had a mixed version of worker self-management. For both political and practical reasons, the state enterprise reform programs in the other socialist countries will not explicitly follow the Yugoslav model. Politically, the other socialist countries will always want to present their efforts as breaking new ground. And given the different national institutions, the other socialist countries will have to find their own way. But the Yugoslav experiment also has not been a great success so there will be resistance to emulating the Yugoslav experiment for pragmatic reasons.

There is no single reason for the difficulties in the Yugoslavian economy. But one cluster of reasons is the weakness of property rights in the self-managed firms ("social property") and the continuing pervasive role of the state and party in the affairs of the enterprise.

In the last two chapters, we have considered some of the ideas and forces in the socialist enterprise programs that are driving towards a worker self-managed socialist model. But given the unclarity over "What is Socialism?" it is also likely that the socialist enterprise reforms will evolve towards a social property model—whose deficiencies have long been evident in Yugoslavia. In this chapter, we chart the evolution of the reforms toward that social property compromise, and then show how the property rights can be resolved without "social property" but within the tradition of self-managed socialism—broadly interpreted as a democratic form of private (i.e. non-governmental) enterprise.

Evolution of the Socialist Enterprise Reform Programs

Collective Contracts

In spite of national differences, there seem to be some common evolutionary forms emerging in the various socialist enterprise reform programs.

One rudimentary form is the *collective contract* similar to the autonomous work teams in the West. A group of workers makes a collective contract with their enterprise and they are paid according to their result. In countries with little social memory of entrepreneurial activity, the collective contract begins the process of workers assuming more legal self-responsibility. But the workers have not assumed true residual claimancy. They do not buy their inputs or sell their outputs. The collective contract is still employment for pay with the pay determined by a collective piece-rate scale.

Enterprise Responsibility Systems

Another initial form might be called the *enterprise responsibility system*. The state enterprises are given a form of market autonomy under management control. They are supposed to be "self-accounting" covering their own losses from their revenues. The roots of the idea go back to the Lerner-Lange model of state-socialist firms simulating decentralizing profit-maximizing firms. The earliest reform using a version of the enterprise responsibility system was the 1968 Hungarian New Economic Mechanism. A similar reform is the centerpiece of the current *perestroika* program embodied in the 1987 State Enterprise Law. The enterprise responsibility system or factory manager contract responsibility system has also been used in the Chinese state sector where the Berle-Means phrase "separation of ownership and control" has even been appropriated to describe the combination of state ownership and decentralized management control.

Reforms such as the collective contract and enterprise responsibility system do promote decentralization and the taste for more autonomy from the center. But they do not change the residual claimant. That is the big step.

Agricultural Family Responsibility Systems

The family farm is one of the oldest forms of the self-managed firm. Leasing the agricultural means of production to family farmers thus creates an institutional arrangement that is a small self-managed firm and also satisfies the ideological need for the government to retain ownership of the means of production. That family responsibility system is the core of Deng Xiaoping's somewhat successful agricultural reforms. Gorbachev is trying a similar reform in the Soviet Union but over a half century of collectivized farming has left little social memory of family farming.

Industrial Enterprise Leasing

How can Deng's success be translated to industry in China or in the other socialist countries? The manager contract responsibility system was the first attempt in China to develop an industrial analogue of the agricultural household contract responsibility system. But it was a poor analogy. In the agricultural case, the workers in the form of the household was the contracting party, and the contract was a lease that shifted residual claimancy to the leasee. That manager contract responsibility system did neither. The manager, not the collectivity of workers, is the contracting party, and the contract is not a lease, so the state remains the residual claimant for the decentralized enterprise as in the Hungarian NEM and the Soviet 1987 Enterprise Law.

The "next" idea is to lease the equipment, industrial factory, and land to the collectivity of workers and managers in the enterprise. That does change residual claimancy to the workers—without changing "government ownership of the means of production." This *enterprise lease* arrangement is now being experimented with in over a thousand firms in the Soviet Union.

The enterprise lease does represent a significant step. Unlike the collective contract or enterprise responsibility arrangements, it changes the residual claimant. In keeping with the tradition of socialism based on "free associations of producers," the new residual claimant is the collectivity of the workers. This reform also raises two important questions.

The first question is about the new corporate form—the legal party leasing the assets from the government. In the Russian lease firms, the legal form of the firm is quite sketchy. It seems to be only a creature of the lease contract which evaporates when the lease expires.

The second question concerns the property rights in the enterprise. Do the members of the collectivity—the workers in the enterprise—have any recoupable capital claim on the net worth of the enterprise? The answer to that question will depend in large part on the strength of the attitudes held over from the other conception of socialism as based on the government ownership of the means of production.

A second question is about the best form of the lease, physical or financial? The initial and most unworkable form of enterprise leasing is a lease of specific physical assets from the government for a limited time period. Quite aside from the first question about legal form and capital claims, this physical lease arrangement is rather problematic. Firstly, workers have little intrinsic motivation for the care and maintenance of leased property—particularly "Government Property." People usually do not lavish great care on a rented car or apartment. Secondly, replacement or new investment expenditures must be made by the government if the point is to retain the "government ownership of the means of production." Such a retention would only have fetishistic value since the government is no longer the residual claimant. Moreover, the transaction costs would be overwhelming in trying to get absentee government bureaucrats in the owner-ministry to implement the capital investment program of a moderately complex industrial enterprise. It is hardly an arrangement that could accommodate the pace of technological change in the late twentieth century.

Financial Leasing?

A more workable alternative would be to transform the physical lease into a financial lease. The enterprise would buy the property rights to the physical means of production from the government with credit supplied by the government. The financial lease or loan could then be serviced and/or amortized over a period of years.

The problem is that the government would "only" be a creditor of the enterprise instead of the owner of the physical fixed assets used by the enterprise. That would be a clear-cut break with the statist conception of socialism in favor of a self-management model. It is precisely that step that is so difficult in today's socialist countries where the Communist Party's monopoly of political power has been based on the state socialist vision. That accounts for the ideological significance of the recent examples in the Soviet Union of moving beyond a worker lease-out to a worker buyout.

Consider an analogy. Under state socialism, the state owns a truck (i.e. the physical enterprise) and the worker (i.e. the collectivity of workers) drives the truck as a state employee. The state is both the owner of the physical asset of the truck and is the residual claimant in the economic operation of the truck. There might be all sorts of arrangements to give the state-employed truck driver more autonomy on the job and to be paid a wage geared to results (e.g. proportional to tonnage hauled). But the real *perestroika* is when the truck driver becomes an independent operator leasing or buying the truck from the state. That changes residual claimancy. The truck operator pays the operating costs (e.g. gas, oil, and maintenance) and is paid by the customers for the tonnage hauled.

Given that important change in residual claimancy, it is another question whether the truck is physically leased to the operator from the state, or the operator purchases the truck on credit supplied by the state (i.e. by a financial lease). The truck operator has better micro-motivation to take care of the truck if he owns the truck (i.e. bought it with a loan) instead of

190

just leases it. Ownership of the truck also facilitates the replacement of the truck and expansion of the operation.

The Social Property Compromise

The "next step" in the evolution of many of the reform programs may be a *Yugoslav-type "social property"* compromise. Instead of government-ownership of specific assets leased to the enterprise, there is a disembodied "social ownership" of the assets used by the enterprise. The enterprise uses the property as trustee for a disembodied "Society." As the property is used up, it must be replaced with new investment of at least equal value. Instead to trying to get government bureaucrats to implement an appropriate capital investment program, the enterprise will conduct its own capital spending program financed by borrowing or by its own retained earnings. This social-property compromise is more workable than a physical lease and it has been implemented in Yugoslavia where the League of Communists still has a political monopoly. Thus all the socialist enterprise reforms may, sooner or later, have to understand the problems in and the solutions to the social property compromise exhibited in the Yugoslav self-managed firms.

Without special government regulations, there is little incentive to finance investment by retained earnings. Earnings paid out as bonuses are definite property rights in the hands of the workers. Earnings retained to finance investment become social property. Insofar as the workers' self-management is genuine, the workers will have every incentive to force the paying out of profits and the financing of all investment by borrowings. Moreover, workers have an incentive to even pay out depreciation allowances and to also finance new investment by debt. Then the government is moved to intervene and further complicate the irrational investment structure by imposing "capital maintenance requirements" to safeguard "social property" (see Ellerman, 1986b).

Yugoslavs take great pride in their claim to have replaced state socialism with a new model of self-management socialism. But the transition is only partial. "Social property" is the ghost of state ownership that still haunts the Yugoslav self-management model.

There is a technical solution within the framework of labor-based self-management, namely, the system of internal capital accounts pioneered by the Mondragon worker cooperatives. But the problem is not simply a technical problem. It is also an ideological problem, the problem of exorcising the ghost of state socialism. But since we have already analyzed the first principles behind the labor-based democratic firm, we turn to the property rights questions that have plagued the socialist enterprise reforms. By combining internal capital accounts with a labor-based democratic structure, the democratic firm has rational investment incentives and definite property rights (often thought to be unique to the capitalist firm) at the same time that it is a democratic social institution.

Property Rights Analysis of the Socialist Reforms

The Liabilities Cancellation Metaphor

We must first consider some common metaphors that often cloud the understanding of property rights. For example, suppose that a person takes out a $40,000 loan from a bank to buy a $60,000 house with a $20,000 down payment, and that the house serves as collateral for the loan. As the person pays off the loan, it is often said that "the person is buying the house from the bank."

Assets	Liabilities
$60,000 House	$40,000 Bank Debt
	$20,000 "Equity" in House

House 100% owned by person.

Figure 10.3 Person's Balance Sheet

192

Does the bank own the house to the extent that the loan is not paid off? Does the bank start off owning two-thirds of the house? No, the person owns 100 per cent of the house from the moment of purchase, and the person *also* holds a liability to the bank for the remaining balance on the loan.

If the $40,000 value of the bank debt is subtracted from the $60,000 value of the house, the resulting $20,000 is sometimes said to be the person's "equity" in the house. But that is only a cancellation of value, not a cancellation of property rights. The person does not just own $20,000 worth or one-third of the house, and the bank does not own the other two-thirds. The person owns 100 per cent of the house and owes a debt to the bank that is initially equal in value to two-thirds of the house.

The manner of speaking and/or thinking of the bank as owning two-thirds the house is the metaphor of *liabilities cancellation*. Value is confused with ownership. The value cancellation $60,000 - $40,000 = $20,000 is misinterpreted as an ownership cancellation leaving the person with only one-third ownership of the house. The bank's claim *against the person* is misinterpreted as a (equal-valued) direct ownership claim on the house—in effect, cancelling the (non-bankrupt) person out of that relationship.

The metaphorical nature of the liabilities cancellation becomes clear upon considering the other attributes of ownership. Only the person has the use rights of the house—to live in it, modify it, or to rent it out to another party. Similarly as the value of the house appreciates, the person gets 100 per cent of the capital gains. The person's use and disposal rights over the house are limited only by the house serving as collateral for the loan. For instance, if the person wanted to sell the house, then the loan would have to be paid off or an acceptable substitute collateral would have to be provided.

The liabilities cancellation metaphor is often used by Western economists in describing the property rights of the residual claimant. The residual claimant owns 100 per cent of the outputs (e.g. the produced assets Q in the example in Chapter 1) and owes 100 per cent of the liabilities for the used-up inputs (e.g. the liabilities for the used-up K and L). Yet the input suppliers' claims against the residual claimant are often "pictured" as being a direct ownership claim on "shares of the product" while the so-called "residual claimant" is pictured as having the claim only on the remaining residual. That is the *distributive shares metaphor*. It applies liabilities cancellation to the income statement while the previous house mortgage example applied it to the balance sheet.

The liabilities cancellation is also used in the socialist argument that "Society" (an abstraction with varying definitions) owns most of the product on the assumption that Society supplies most of the capital and other inputs to production. The workers get a certain share of the product and that is paid out as wages and bonuses. The rest of the product belongs to Society since Society supplied the other inputs.

This argument mistakes the structure of property rights as well as the structure of the labor theory of property argument for the worker-managed firm. Even granting, for the sake of argument, that "Society" supplies most or all the other inputs, it does not follow that Society should own part of the outputs. It follows that the residual claimant is *liable to Society* for those inputs. In other words, instead of having a direct claim on the product, Society as an input supplier has a claim against the residual claimant.

The labor theory of property argues furthermore that Labor, the workers in the enterprise, should be that residual claimant. Thus the labor theory does not "ignore the claims of Society"; it simply does not misinterpret those claims as direct ownership claims on the product. Labor must satisfy its liabilities for using up the inputs supplied by "Society."

In addition, state socialists tend to misunderstand the structure of property rights by accepting the Fundamental Myth (see Chapter 1) that residual claimancy is part of the "ownership of the means of production." Thus given that Society starts off owning the means of production, state socialists conclude that Society should be the residual claimant. But residual claimancy is not inherently tied to capital as shown by the leasing arrangement which separates residual claimancy from capital ownership. The labor theory implies that Labor should be liable to the owner of the means of production for using the services of that capital.

Another question clouded by the liabilities cancellation metaphor is the question of who owns the assets of a corporation. In the example of the homeowner, take the person to be the legal person of a corporation. A party to whom the corporation owes a liability (such as the bank) does not own any portion of the corporate assets. Like the person in the example, the corporation owns 100 per cent of its assets.

In a democratic corporation with internal capital accounts, the workers do not own the corporate assets. The democratic firm is a social institution with the workers as its "citizens" or members. The internal capital accounts are "internal" debt capital analogous to the national debt owed by a country to its citizens. Those liabilities should not be "cancelled" and misinterpreted as direct ownership claims on the assets. The workers do not own the corporate physical assets any more than citizens holding treasury bonds or government savings bonds own government property.

The "Two Pockets" Principle

It is no surprise that Western commentators tend to consider the capitalist corporation as the only alternative to the property-rights deficient state-owned or socially-owned firm. Even some of the more "liberal" socialist commentators take the capitalist property structure as the only alternative. Hence we will organize our analysis by considering some of the capitalist recommendations made for the socialist reforms and then by showing how the democratic firm addresses those concerns.

As state enterprises become more autonomous (e.g. with the enterprise responsibility reforms) and workers gain more formal or real power (e.g. enterprise councils or worker councils), then pressure will increase on managers to pay out more of revenues and even reserves to workers as pay, bonuses, and benefits. As Gorbachev has noted "...socialist property...became nobody's property, having no real owner" (quoted in Schroeder, 1988, p. 181)—while property paid out (or stolen) became somebody's property. That has always been true in state enterprises in the East and West, but with the decentralizing reforms managers become much more vulnerable to worker pressure to decapitalize the enterprise.

Western commentators advise the solution of having private or perhaps non-governmental institutional owners of the enterprises. The new owners need a strong enough interest in the capital assets of the enterprise to resist the worker demands for higher payouts and decapitalization of the enterprise. Thus some form of the capitalist corporation is presented as the *only* solution to the property rights deficiencies ("nobody's property") of the state firm.

The owners of a capitalist corporation can also pay out cash to themselves—namely as dividends. Why don't *they* just decapitalize the company? The owners also gain or lose value from the company through the capital gains or losses in their share value. They have "two pockets" instead of one. Money they pay out as dividends goes into one pocket but they suffer a corresponding loss in the capital value of the company—so the money comes out of their other pocket. That is as it should be. Since it is their wealth either way, whether the wealth is in one pocket or the other, the owners can then make the pay-out-or-retain decision according to the financial opportunities outside or inside the company.

That same two pockets principle applies to the democratic firm with internal capital accounts. The members' capital accounts are their second pockets. Retained profits add to the balances in the accounts, and paid out profits subtract from (or refrain from adding to) those accounts.

Worker's Pocket: Member's Pocket:
Value of   Value of
Wages   Capital Account

Figure 10.4   Worker-Member's "Two Pockets"

Thus the worker-members get the wealth either way; it is a question of the relative opportunities available inside and outside the firm.

For the workers, it is not simply a question of financial rate of return since the company is their job. With the "hard budget constraint" of potential bankruptcy, the workers would harm themselves in two way by decapitalizing the company—by reducing the value of their capital accounts and by jeopardizing their own livelihoods.

The structure of this argument is instructive. The property-deficient socialist firm violates the two-pockets principle. The capitalist firm satisfies the principle. Hence capitalist economists and many reformers in socialist countries conclude that the only solution is the capitalist firm. A similar thought-pattern is repeated over and over again in the socialist reform debates. Capitalist economics has little interest in analyzing the underlying principle (such as the "two-pockets principle") and showing how it could also be satisfied in non-capitalist firms. We will see how the same thought-pattern is repeated in the debate over capital markets.

While both the capitalist and the democratic structures solve the property rights problem using the two pockets principle, the capitalist firm as well as the state firm involves the motivational inefficiency (or "X-inefficiency") of the employer–employee relation. The managers and workers have no intrinsic motivation when employed by absentee share-holders or a state ministry. This is referred to in the Western literature as "agency costs"—the costs incurred by the principal or employer to motivate and monitor the agents or employees as well as the costs of the suboptimal performance on the part of the agents and employees.

It is interesting to notice some variation in the labelling of problems depending on the ideological undertones. When Soviet managers and workers do not husband and conserve the property of a state firm, that is called a "property rights deficiency" in the Western literature. When American managers and workers in a large corporation with publicly traded shares treat the corporate property in the same manner, that is called an "agency problem." Yet by any objective measure, the "property rights" enjoyed by a Soviet ministry over an enterprise are a good deal stronger than the rights held by the dispersed absentee shareholders of a large American corporation. But if the Soviet difficulties were also called "agency problems" that would set up an uncomfortable analogy between the absentee-owned companies of the East and West.

Self-management drastically reduces, if not eliminates, certain agency costs. For instance, one economic actor who is self-managing in Western economies is the consumer. There is no "incentives problem" to motivate the consumer to maximize his or her utility. There is no "agency problem" to supervise and monitor the consumer to insure the maximization of utility. In the democratic firm, the collectivity of the worker-members is self-managing, and thus there is no *collective* incentive or agency problem.

There is still the classic divergence of interests between the individual and the collective. Consider the problem of worker pilfering or theft of company property. If *everyone* stole $100 a year then in addition to the damage to company *esprit de corps* and self-discipline, there would be no economic gain since the workers would get a corresponding $100 loss to their capital accounts. But if one person steals $100 and everyone else refrains, then the thief gets the exclusive benefit while the loss is spread over all the group.

Thus the self-management structure with capital accounts gives proper collective motivation but does not automatically solve the old divergence between individual and collective interests in a democratic organization. There is some evidence, and certainly some hope, that the correct collective incentives will become individualized through horizontal monitoring between worker-members ("Hey, you're taking money out of my pocket!"), but that mechanism is far from automatic. In a private or public enterprise capitalist firm, the employees do not even have a collective incentive (not to mention individual incentives) to preserve and maintain "company property"—and old habits die hard.

Is an Equity Market Necessary for Efficient Capital Allocation?

There are two allocation problems that need to be considered separately: the allocation of capital (physical and financial), and the allocation of risk. Capital allocation is discussed in this section and risk allocation in the next.

198

Both types of allocation are involved in the stock market—that universal symbol of capitalism in both the capitalist and socialist worlds. In spite of the stock market's large symbolic value, it is notorious that it has relatively little to do with the production of goods and services in the economy (the gambling industry aside). The overwhelming bulk of stock transactions are in second-hand shares so the capital paid for shares usually goes to other stock traders, not to productive enterprises issuing new shares.

The "stock market" has nevertheless been prominent in the socialist reform debates—apparently due to its pull on the popular imagination. Socialist reformers in countries without even a decentralized banking system for small or medium-sized firms think that having a "stock market" will somehow solve their problems of business development.

Our concern is with the more sophisticated arguments by economists that a stock market is necessary for the efficient allocation of capital. Socialist firms are routinely attacked as being inherently inefficient because they have no equity shares exposed to market valuation. If this argument had any merit, it would imply that the whole sector of unquoted closely-held small and medium-sized firms in the West was "inherently inefficient"—a conclusion that must be viewed with some skepticism. Indeed, in the comparison to large corporations with publicly-traded shares, the closely-held firms are probably *more* efficient users of capital. At the level of pure theory, the fundamental theorem in neo-classical economics, i.e. the theorem that a competitive equilibrium is allocatively efficient, is formulated in a model without a stock market (see Quirk and Saposnik, 1968).

Where has the argument gone wrong? Doesn't the absence of a market spell inefficiency? It always seems useful to consider the analogy with slavery and its abolition. Is a market economy inherently inefficient after the abolition of slavery since that eliminates slave markets? *Given* that workers are legally treated as property, a market in such property would promote efficiency of allocation (as opposed to a bureaucratic allocation mechanism). But efficiency does not imply that there must be slavery in the first place. When slavery is abolished, then efficiency requires some other means for the allocation of work that pays due regard for the valuation of alternative applications of work. A slave market is not a necessary condition for the efficient allocation of work.

In a similar manner, *given* that productive enterprises are treated as property expressed in equity shares, a market in such property would promote efficiency of allocation. But efficiency does not require that enterprises be treated as property in the first place.

For a closer examination of the argument, we must distinguish between two quite different types of "capital markets"—neither of which exists in socialist countries. One is the group of markets in physical and financial capital—the market in the "means of productions" as well as the financial loan market. The other is the market in equity shares—the stock market.

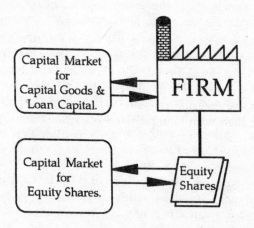

Figure 10.5 Two Different Kinds of Capital Markets

The efficient allocation of capital in production does not require a stock market (witness the small business sector). But it does require a market in capital goods and loan capital or some equivalent mechanism so that the scarcity value of physical and financial capital will be reflected in decisions about its allocation.

How does the efficient allocation of capital take place at the level of the firm? A proposed capital project is analyzed.

Given the scarcity-reflecting cost of the capital goods and other inputs involved, the rate of return over cost is computed to see if it compares favorably with the interest costs of borrowing funds to finance the project. Even if the project could be self-financed, the interest cost of borrowing or lending money gives the benchmark opportunity cost of tying down the funds in the project. This project analysis requires a scarcity value for the capital goods and for the loan capital, and thus it requires a capital market (or some equivalent mechanism) for those items.

A market in the second-hand equity shares of the company is, by itself, quite irrelevant to the analysis of the capital project. For a firm to investigate the profitability of using a new widget-maker machine, it must know the value of the machine, not the value of its own second-hand shares or the value of the shares in the company making widget-maker machines. Potential capital projects can be analyzed quite well in closely-held corporations with no market in their equity shares. A stock market would only be relevant if floating new shares offered an alternative source of funding. That source would hardly be cheaper since shareholders must be additionally compensated for bearing more risk. A stock market does allow for some external risk-sharing and thus a better allocation of risk than with straight fixed-interest loan capital. But as we will see in the next section, such an allocation of risk can be obtained without the specifically capitalist tool of marketable equity shares.

Some socialist reformers have suggested a "socialist stock market" with pension funds, institutions, and other enterprises as the principal stock traders. In that manner, the problem of "valuing capital" would supposedly be solved. But a stock market would not be a substitute for the market to value capital goods and loan capital, and we have seen that it is the markets for physical and financial capital that provide the information necessary to evaluate capital projects and to efficiently allocate capital. It might be answered that markets in physical and financial capital do not provide a market value for equity shares; only a stock market can do that. And only a slave market can provide a market value for slaves.

Another argument is that a stock market is necessary so that economic performance will be reflected in the value of property. But the internal capital accounts in democratic firms perform that function without having marketable equity shares.

In a market economy of democratic firms (without hired labor), there can be full markets in capital goods and loan capital. Thus the labor income, determined as the revenues minus the non-labor costs, is available as an indicator of the efficient use of material resources. If an accounting wage is assigned to labor, then the labor income can be divided into the wage and the remaining "pure profit."

In a market economy of capitalist corporations, retained profits add to stock value. In democratic firms, retained profits add to the value in the capital accounts just as deposited wages add to a worker's savings account in a bank. In *both* cases, retained profits add to the capital value in someone's pocket. The differences lie elsewhere.

The capitalist company is itself a piece of property represented by the equity shares, and the market value of those shares reflects the economic fundamentals of profit and losses—as well as psychological and speculative elements on the stock market.

The democratic firm is a social institution, not a piece of property. Thus it has no free-floating "market value" any more than does a town or city—even though the particular assets owned by a town or city might have a market value. The internal capital accounts are a flexible form of debt capital. Retained profits or losses are credited or debited to those accounts so the capital value of the accounts is a property right that directly reflects the economic fundamentals of profit and loss. Thus property rights can reflect economic performance without having the firm itself being a piece of property with a free-floating market value.

Is an Equity Market Necessary for Efficient Risk Allocation?

The internal capital accounts in democratic firms establish the two pockets principle so there are rational investment incentives and efficient performance will be reflected in capital values. But capital accounts, by themselves, do not promote efficient *risk* allocation.

A public capital market in salable or negotiable securities is one of the remarkable social inventions of capitalism. How can it be adapted to an economic democracy? "Securities" refers to both debt and equity instruments. Worker-owned companies or consortia of such firms may issue negotiable debt instruments such as bonds and debentures.

The correlation between membership and work in a firm will not be maintained if the workers can freely sell their equity rights while still working in the firm. There is one reason why traditional equity instruments do not mix well with worker ownership. Let us review the capital structure of a conventional corporation. Control (e.g. to elect the board of directors) is attached to the common voting shares with a non-mandatory payout (i.e. dividends). Control is not attached to the debt instruments with mandatory interest payments. That makes sense. If the holders of corporate debt have no control rights, then the payout to them must be obligatory.

Non-voting preferred stock is "dequity," an intermediate security between debt and equity. Like debt it has no vote, but like equity it has no mandatory payout. However, preferred stock still has a value because it is "piggy-backed" onto the common stock dividends. Dividends up to a certain percentage of face value must be paid on preferred stock before any common stock dividends can be paid. Preferred stockholders do not need control rights since they can assume the common stockholders will attend to their own interests.

The preferred stockholders are like tax collectors that charge their tax on any value the common stockholders take out the front door. But that valuation theory breaks down if the common stockholders have a *back door*—a way to extract value from the company without paying the tax to the preferred stockholders. That is the situation in a worker-owned company where the worker-members can always take their value out the "back door" of wages, bonuses, and benefits. A similar problem exists in the large management-dominated corporations where the back door is managerial salaries, bonuses, stock options, and other perquisites.

As noted in Chapter 3, the back door problem can be resolved using a "dequity" security, a non-voting, variable income security called a *profit-sharing security* or a *participating security* since the capital supplier "shares the profits" or "participates in the variable income" of the enterprise.

For instance, a participating bond or debenture would have two or more levels of interest. There is a minimum level of interest which then "kicks up" to a higher level if the firm has certain pre-specified levels of value-added or total labor income. The payout is *mandatory* so it avoids the back door problem. The payout is *variable* so it involves risk-sharing with outside capital suppliers. When value-added falls, the capital cost to the firm and the return to the participating bond-holders falls so risk has been shared. Thus participating securities provide a mechanism for the efficient allocation of risks without a market in equity shares.

Is it practical? For *small* shareholders, the equity shares in the public stock markets in the United States are *already* a form of profit-sharing securities. With the separation of ownership and control in the large quoted corporations, the vote is of little use to small shareholders. Dividends are discretionary in theory but are quasi-mandatory in practice. The "missed dividend" is the exception that proves the rule, and the root cause is the similar back door problem of managerial salaries and perquisites. Hence for small shareholders, "equity shares" already function like non-voting, variable income, perpetual securities with quasi-mandatory payouts, i.e. as participating dequity securities. Hence *a priori* arguments that public capital markets in participating dequity securities are not workable must be viewed with some skepticism.

With a market in non-voting participating securities replacing equity shares, the small capital-suppliers would hardly notice the difference and the large capital-suppliers would not be able to mount takeover bids. Democratic firms would be able to focus their attention on producing better goods and services instead of improving their takeover defenses. External takeovers are as inappropriate for democratic firms as they are for other democratic polities. It is symptomatic of the moral condition of corporate capitalism that external takeover raids

204

are seriously proposed as an accountability mechanism for management—the Attila-the-Hun theory of accountability. Democratic firms use another accountability mechanism.

Stock markets in equity shares are a sufficient but not a necessary condition for a more efficient allocation of risk. It seems quite possible to have a vibrant public capital market—with the resulting more efficient allocation of risk—in an economy dominated by democratic worker-owned companies with no marketable equity shares. The securities would be the usual negotiable bonds, debentures, and commercial paper—as well as the special profit-sharing or participating dequity securities.

Conclusion

Economic Democracy as a Third Way

An *economic democracy* can be roughly defined as a mixed market economy where the predominance of economic enterprises are democratic worker-owned firms (see Dahl, 1985). It differs from capitalism primarily in the abolition of the employment relation. The relationship between the worker and the firm is membership, an economic version of "citizenship," not employment. It differs from (state) socialism in that the firms are democratic worker-owned firms, not government-owned firms, and the firms are interrelated by a market economy with various degrees of macro-economic guidance furnished by the government.

Economic democracy is a genuine third way that is structurally different from classical capitalism and socialism. It can be viewed as an outcome of evolution starting either from capitalism or from socialism.

A capitalist economy within a political democracy can evolve to an economy of economic democracy by extending the principle of democratic self-determination to the workplace. It would be viewed by many as the perfection of capitalism since it replaces the demeaning employer–employee relationship with ownership and co-entrepreneurship for all the workers.

A state socialist economy can evolve into an economic democracy by restructuring itself along the lines of the self-management socialist tradition. It would be viewed by many as the perfection of socialism since the workers would finally become masters of their own destiny in firms organized as free associations of producers.

There is more to an economy and certainly more to a socio-political system than the form of economic enterprise. Yet we have intentionally focused only on the firm—not on broader economic or social questions. This has been quite feasible due to the traditional neglect of the firm in both capitalist and

206

socialist economic theory. In neo-classical economics, the firm is seen as a technologically specified black-box or, from the institutional viewpoint, as a piece of property, a capital asset—not a community of work qualifying for democracy. Socialist theory, from Marx onwards, has been notoriously silent about the "socialist firm."

First Principles

The Labor Theory of Property

The democratic firm is grounded on first principles, the twin pillars of the labor theory of property and democratic theory.

The analysis began by setting aside what we called the "Fundamental Myth" that residual claimancy is part of the ownership of the means of production. The whole question of the ownership of the new assets and liabilities created in production (which accrue to the residual claimant) has been suppressed in capitalist economics because those assets and liabilities were taken as part of the already-existing owner-ship of the means of production. By simply considering the case where the physical means of production are rented or leased, we can see that the residual claimant appropriating those new produced assets and liabilities could be different from the owner of the means of production. The ownership of the capital used in production only determines to whom the residual claimant is liable for the used-up services of capital.

Having conceptually separated the residual claimant's role from the capital supplier's role, we then turned to the normative question of who ought to appropriate those new assets and liabilities created in production. We applied the standard juridical principle that legal responsibility should be assigned to the *de facto* responsible party. Regardless of the causal efficacy of the services of capital and land, only the intentional actions of persons can be *de facto* responsible for anything. Thus the people involved in a productive enterprise, the managers and workers, are *de facto* responsible for produc-ing the outputs and for using up the inputs. By the standard juridical principle, they should therefore have the legal liability for the used-up inputs and the legal ownership of the produced outputs, i.e. they ought to be the residual claimant.

This argument is none other than the old "labor theory of property" usually associated with John Locke restated in modern terms using the language of jurisprudence. The argument also makes sense out the peculiar dual life that Locke's theory has always had; it is taken as the basis of private property as well as the basis for a radical critique of capitalist production. We found that there was no contradiction in that outcome. Labor is the natural foundation for private property appropriation, and capitalist production—far from being "founded on private property"—denies that labor basis for appropriation. In that sense, it is private property itself that calls for the abolition of capitalist production (i.e. the employment relation) so that people will always appropriate the positive and negative fruits of their labor.

This same idea occurs in a rather oblique form in the socialist tradition as the "labor theory of value." The labor theory of value has always had two rather different interpretations: labor as a measure of value, and labor as a "source" of value or, rather, of what has value. The measure version of the labor theory of value has been a complete failure—and, in any case, it had no interesting normative implications. Thus capitalist economists want to stick to the measure version of the theory (since it is a failure) and state socialists also want to stick to it (since it has no implications against state socialism). The alternative source version of the "labor theory of value" is the labor theory of property disguised in "value talk." It has direct implications against capitalist production in favor of the democratic firm, and it has direct implications against state socialism in favor of the alternative tradition of democratic self-management socialism.

The end result of this reformulation of the basic issues is that a new "villain" emerges, the employment relation. The villain of capitalist production is not private property or free markets (far from it), but the whole legal relationship of renting, hiring, or employing human beings. It was the employment relation that allowed some other party to hire the workers so that together with the ownership of the other inputs, that party would be the residual claimant.

An old inalienable rights argument, originally developed against the self-sale contract, was applied against the self-rental contract, the employment contract. As illustrated by the example of an employee obeying an order to commit a crime, *de facto* responsible human actions, i.e. labor services, are not factually transferable—so the legal contract to transfer labor is natural-law invalid.

Instead of abolishing the employment relation, state socialism nationalized it. Substituting state ownership of slaves for private ownership would not abolish slavery, and substituting employment of the workers in the name of the "public good" for employment in the interest of "private greed" does not abolish the employment, hiring, or renting of workers.

Only the democratic firm—where the workers are jointly self-employed—is a genuine alternative to private or public employment.

Democratic Theory

The residual claimant has the direct control rights over the production process. The application of democratic principles to work has thus been clouded by the Fundamental Myth that residual claimancy is part of the ownership of the means of production. As the leasing movement in the Soviet Union has discovered, the renting or leasing of capital separates the direct control rights over production from capital ownership.

The ownership of capital only gives the owner an indirect control right, a right to say "No, you may not use the capital," the right to make the worker into a trespasser. To acquire the direct control and authority over workers, the capital owner must also be an employer. Indeed, a "capitalist" is a capital owner who is also an employer. Without the employment relation, a capital owner is not a "capitalist" but is only a capital supplier to worker-managed firms.

The same logic holds when the capital owner is a corporation. Of course, the shareholders have the control rights over the *affairs of the corporation*. But it is the employment contract or its opposite, a capital leasing contract, that determines whether the "affairs of the corporation" include authority over the workers in the production process (when labor is hired in) or simply the leasing out of capital to the workers or some other party undertaking the production process.

Traditional liberalism's inability to significantly raise the question of applying democratic principles to the workplace (see any standard economics text) has been fostered by the public/private distinction. Democracy governs in the "public" sphere while property supposedly governs in the private sphere. But that misinterprets the rights of property. Property only includes the indirect control right, say, to make a worker a trespasser. Authority or direct control over the worker only comes from the employment relation. Property is only relevant as giving the bargaining power to make the employment contract rather than the capital leasing contract.

Capitalist liberalism has also misrepresented the whole question of democratic or non-democratic government in the public sphere as a question of consent or coercion. That is superficial intellectual history (see Ellerman, 1986a) which allows capitalist production to be presented as analogous to public democracy since both are based on consent. Marxists typically miss the point by questioning whether or not capitalist production is "really" voluntary. The real point is that there is a whole liberal tradition of apologizing for non-democratic government based on consent—on a voluntary social contract alienating governance rights to a sovereign, e.g. the Hobbesian *pactum subjectionis*. The employment contract is the modern limited workplace version of that Hobbesian contract.

The critique of capitalist production is a critique of the voluntary employment contract, the individual contract for the renting of people and the collective Hobbesian *pactum subjectionis* for the workplace. The critique is not new; it was developed in the Enlightenment doctrine of inalienable rights. It was applied by abolitionists against the voluntary self-enslavement contract and by political democrats against the voluntary contractarian defense of non-democratic government.

Today's economic democrats are the *new abolitionists* trying to abolish the whole institution of renting people in favor of democratic self-management in the workplace.

It might be noted that we have purposely refrained from emphasizing the efficiency arguments customarily used in favor of the democratic firm. Both capitalism and state socialism suffer from the motivational inefficiency of the employment relation. Thus efficiency provides the principal "practical" reason for the two-sided evolution in the direction of greater participation and democracy in the workplace.

But efficiency considerations always leave the structure of rights under-determined. If it is only efficiency that counts, then non-democratic structures can always be designed to try to *simulate* participative democratic structures (e.g. profit-sharing and participation programs in capitalist firms). If a simulation fails, then there will always be other variations that might provide a better simulation.

Real social change, when it comes, is driven by ideas and principles, not simply by "efficiency considerations." Absolute government as well as slavery sagged after centuries of inefficiency, but it was their illegitimacy in the light of first principles that drove the democratic revolutions and the abolition of slavery in the eighteenth and nineteenth centuries. Thus we have focused on the basic principles that drive towards economic democracy.

The Democratic Firm

The democratic firm was defined by showing how the conventional bundle of ownership rights is restructured and reassigned so as to satisfy democratic theory and the labor theory of property.

Democratic theory is implemented in an organization by treating the ultimate direct control rights, i.e. the voting rights to elect the board, as personal rights assigned to the functional role of being governed.

The labor theory of property is implemented by assigning the rights to the produced outputs and the liabilities for the used-up inputs whose net value is the residual or net income to the functional role of working in the enterprise.

Thus the twin pillars of democratic theory and the labor theory of property imply that the two membership rights, the voting and profit rights, should be assigned as personal rights to the functional role of working in the firm. Since the membership rights become personal rights, the democratic firm becomes a democratic social institution rather than the traditional piece of property.

The remaining rights to the net value of the corporate assets and liabilities remain property rights represented in the internal capital accounts. The individual accounts represent property originally put in by the workers (e.g. membership fees) and the net value of the fruits of their labor reinvested in the firm.

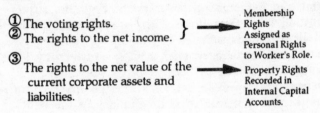

Figure 11.1 Restructured Ownership Bundle in a Democratic Firm

The system of internal capital accounts is not an afterthought. It is an integral part of the structure that corrects the property rights deficiencies of "social property" involved in the self-managed socialist firm.

Worker-owned Companies in the USA and Europe

The best examples of democratic firms in the world today are the worker cooperatives in the Mondragon group of the Basque country in Spain. One of their important social inventions is the system of internal capital accounts which they pioneered over the last quarter century. There are new worker cooperative statutes in the United States and United Kingdom that reflect the Mondragon-type structure.

Another major example of worker ownership in the West is the employee stock ownership plan or ESOP developed in the United States over the last 15 years and just starting in the United Kingdom. The ESOPs have been heavily promoted in America with tax advantages so that there are now about 10,000 ESOPs covering about 10 per cent of the workforce. ESOPs have also been controversial because they are usually management-dominated. Workers get the financial aspects of "ownership" without the control aspects, so ESOPs tend to create a new "second class" category of ownership for workers.

The ideology of ESOP promoters has been heavily worker capitalist. But the origin of ESOPs in pension law gives them many labor-based aspects—so there is some irony in the worker capitalist ideology. The real innovation of the ESOP is allowing the workers to use the leverage of the company to take out a loan to buy stock, and then to have the company pay back the loan as a tax deductible expense. The ESOP also allows the slow conversion of a company to worker ownership whereas traditional cooperative forms were not easily hybridizable.

The lessons of the Mondragon-type worker cooperative and of the democratic ESOP were combined in a new model, the *hybrid democratic firm*, which could be implemented in other countries of the East and West.

The Socialist Enterprise Reform Programs

These are interesting and exciting times in the socialist world; the economic and political forms of state socialism are breaking down. Although interpreted in the West as a reversion to capitalism, it is more plausibly seen as an evolution away from state socialism to a market system of self-management socialism.

The current *perestroika* in the Soviet Union, the system reforms in China, the renaissance of markets in Hungary, and the development of Solidarity and the self-management idea in Poland are evolving—with zigs and zags—in the direction of democratic worker ownership. Yugoslavia, since the 1950s, has developed a form of worker self-management that has been haunted by the ghost of state socialism in the form of "social property." Yugoslavia is now evolving towards a new model of mixed economy where worker self-management is coupled with worker ownership.

The democratic firm with internal capital accounts is a model for the self-managed socialist firm that corrects the property rights deficiencies of the social property firm.

The Democratic Firm and East/West Convergence

In the West, democracy will not forever remain alien to "what people do all day long." Even without explicit worker ownership, many firms in the capitalist world (including Japan) are evolving in the direction of recognizing the workforce as the primary stakeholders or "owners" of the firm. The ESOPs and other worker-owned companies are only the tip of the iceberg in this long-term trend in the direction of the democratic firm.

In the socialist world, the very concept of "socialism" is evolving away from the socialism of the state towards a market model of decentralized socialism with self-management in the workplace. The democratic firm is the new developing model of the "private" socialist firm.

The East and West are thus converging towards the common ground of the democratic worker-owned firm.

References

Adams, Frank and Hansen, Gary 1987. *Putting Democracy to Work: A Practical Guide for Starting Worker-owned Businesses.* Eugene, OR: Hulogos'i Press.

Aganbegyan, Abel 1988. *The Economic Challenge of Perestroika.* Translated by Pauline Tiffen. Bloomington: Indiana University Press.

Bárony, J. 1982. Tibor Liska's Concept of Socialist Entrepreneurship. *Acta Oeconomica.* 28 (3–4), 422–55.

Batt, Francis 1967. *The Law of Master and Servant.* 5th ed. Edited by G. Webber. London: Pitman.

Bellas, C.J. 1972. *Industrial Democracy and the Worker Owned Firm.* New York: Praeger.

Berle, A. and Means, G. 1967. *The Modern Corporation and Private Property.* Revised edition. New York: Harcourt, Brace & World (orig. published 1932).

Berman, K. 1967. *Worker-owned Plywood Companies.* Pullman: Washington State University Press.

Blasi, Joseph R. 1988. *Employee Ownership: Revolution or Ripoff?* Cambridge: Ballinger.

Bonin, J. and Putterman, L. 1987. *Economics of Cooperation and Labor-managed Economy.* London: Harwood.

Brealey, Richard and Myers, Stewart 1984. *Principles of Corporate Finance.* Second Edition. New York: McGraw-Hill.

Brown, Douglas M. 1988. *Towards a Radical Democracy: The Political Economy of the Budapest School.* London: Unwin Hyman.

Cassirer, Ernst 1963. *The Myth of the State.* New Haven: Yale University Press.

Catterall, Helen T. 1926. *Judicial Cases Concerning Slavery and the Negro.* Vol. III. Washington, DC: Carnegie Institution of Washington.

Chayes, Abram 1966. The Modern Corporation and the Rule of Law. In E. S. Mason (ed.). *The Corporation in Modern Society.* New York: Atheneum.

Cohen, G.A. 1981. The Labour Theory of Value and the Concept of Exploitation. In *The Value Controversy.* London: Verso, 202–23.

Cole, G.D.H. 1920. *Guild Socialism Re-stated.* London: Leonard Parsons.

215

Dabrowski, Marek 1988. *The Level of Enterprise Autonomy in Different Variants of Economic Reforms in Socialist Countries.* Mimeo. Warsaw: Institute of Economic Sciences.

Dahl, Robert 1985. *Preface to Economic Democracy.* Berkeley: University of California Press.

Deliusin, Lev P. 1988. Reforms in China: Problems and Prospects. *Asian Survey.* XXVIII (11) : 1101–16.

Dobb, Maurice 1973. *Theories of Value and Distribution since Adam Smith.* Cambridge: Cambridge University Press.

Donaldson, Elvin and Pfahl, John 1963. *Corporate Finance.* Second edition. New York: Ronald Press.

Ellerman, David P. 1982. *Economics, Accounting, and Property Theory.* Lexington MA: D.C. Heath.

Ellerman, David P. 1983. Marxian Exploitation Theory: A Brief Exposition, Analysis and Critique. *Philosophical Forum,* Vol. XIV, No. 3–4, (Spring–Summer 1983), 315–33.

Ellerman, David P. 1984a. Entrepreneurship in the Mondragon Cooperatives. *Review of Social Economy.* Vol. XLII, No. 3 (Dec. 1984), 272–94.

Ellerman, David P. 1984b. *Management Planning with Labor as a Fixed Cost: The Mondragon Annual Business Plan Manual.* Somerville, MA: Industrial Cooperative Association.

Ellerman, David P. 1985a. On the Labor Theory of Property. *The Philosophical Forum.* No. 4, Vol. XVI (Summer 1985), 293–326.

Ellerman, David P. 1985b. *Worker Ownership: Economic Democracy or Worker Capitalism?* Somerville MA: Industrial Cooperative Association.

Ellerman, David P. 1986a. The Employment Contract and Liberal Thought. *Review of Social Economy,* Vol. XLIV, No.1 (April 1986) 13–39.

Ellerman, David P. 1986b. Horizon Problems and Property Rights in Labor-Managed Firms. *The Journal of Comparative Economics,* 10 (March 1986) 62–78.

Ellerman, David P. 1988a. Democratic Worker Ownership: A Model for China. *Reform (Beijing),* Issue 2, No. 28, March 1988 (in Chinese).

Ellerman, David P. 1988b. The Legitimate Opposition at Work: The Union's Role in Large Democratic Firms. *Economic and Industrial Democracy: An International Journal.* Vol. 9, No. 4 (Nov. 1988), 437–53.

Ellerman, David P. 1988c. The Kantian Person/Thing Principle in Political Economy, *Journal of Economic Issues.* Vol. 22 (4) (Dec. 1988), 1109–22.

216

Ellerman, David P. 1989a. The Internal ESOP: ESOP Transactions without an External Trust. *Proceedings of Twelth Annual Convention.* Washington, DC: The ESOP Association.

Ellerman, David P. 1989b. *Foundations of Economic Democracy.* Unpublished book manuscript.

Ellerman, David P. 1989c. *The Internal Democratic ESOP.* Somerville, MA: Employee Ownership Services.

Ellerman, D. and Pitegoff, Peter 1983. The Democratic Corporation: The New Worker Cooperative Statute in Massachusetts. *NYU Review of Law and Social Change.* Vol. XI No. 3. (Winter), 441–72.

Estrin, S. 1983. *Self-management: Economic Theory and Yugoslav Practice.* Cambridge: Cambridge University Press.

Fischer, Stanley, Rudiger Dornbusch, and Richard Schmalensee. 1988. Economics. 2nd ed. New York: McGraw-Hill Co.

Furubotn, E., and S. Pejovich 1970. Property Rights and the Behavior of the Firm in a Socialist State: The Example of Yugoslavia. *Zeitschrift fur Nationalokonomie.* 30 (3–4): 431–54.

Furubotn, E., and Pejovich, S. (eds.) 1974. *The Economics of Property Rights.* Cambridge: Ballinger.

Gierke, Otto von 1966. *The Development of Political Theory.* Trans. B. Freyd. New York: Howard Fertig.

Goodell, William. 1969 (Orig. 1853). *The American Slave Code in Theory and Practice.* New York: New American Library.

Gorbachev, Mikhail 1988a. *Perestroika: New Thinking for Our Country and the World.* New York: Harper & Row.

Gorbachev, Mikhail 1988b. Gorbachev Asks Wide-Scale Farm Leasing. *Current Digest of the Soviet Press.* XL (41): 1–6.

Henderson, James P. 1985. An English Communist, Mr. Bray [and] his remarkable work. *History of Political Economy.* Vol. 17, 1 (1985), 73–95.

Hiltzik, Michael 1985. Employee stock plans turn into management boon. *The Boston Globe.* January 2, 1985.

Hobson, S.G. 1919. *National Guilds: An Inquiry into the Wage System and the Way Out.* London: G. Bell & Sons Ltd.

Hodgskin, Thomas 1827. *Popular Political Economy.* Reprinted in 1966, New York.

Hodgskin, Thomas 1832. *The Natural and Artificial Right of Property Contrasted.* Reprinted in 1973. Clifton: Augustus M. Kelley.

Holland, David C. 1988. Workers' Self-Management Before and After 1981. In P. Marer and W. Siwinski (eds). *Creditworthiness and Reform in Poland,* 133–41. Bloomington: Indiana University Press.

Horvat, Branko, Mihailo Markovic, and Rudi Supek (eds.) 1975. *Self-governing Socialism*. White Plains: International Arts and Sciences Press.

Hsu, Robert C. 1988. Economics and Economists in Post-Mao China. *Asian Survey*. XXVIII (12) : 1211–28.

ICA 1984. *ICA Model By-laws for a Worker Cooperative: Version II*. Somerville MA: Industrial Cooperative Association.

Jiang, Yiwei 1988. *From Enterprise-Based Economy to Economic Democracy*. Beijing: Beijing Review Press.

Kelso, Louis 1967. *How to Turn Eighty Million Workers Into Capitalists on Borrowed Money*. New York: Random House.

Kelso, Louis 1988a. *ESOPs Readings in Binary Economics: The Foundation of the ESOP*. San Francisco: Kelso & Company.

Kelso, Louis 1988b. *Preface*. In *Fair Shares for All the Workers*. By I. Taylor. 1–5. London: Adam Smith Institute.

Kelso, Louis and Adler, Mortimer 1958. *The Capitalist Manifesto*. New York: Random House.

Kelso, Louis and Hetter, Patricia 1967. *Two-Factor Theory: The Economics of Reality*. New York: Vintage Books.

Kelso, Louis and Kelso, Patricia Hetter 1986. *Democracy and Economic Power*. Cambridge: Ballinger.

King, J.E. 1983. Utopian or scientific? A reconsideration of the Ricardian Socialists. *History of Political Economy*. 15:3, 345–73.

Knight, Frank H. 1965. *Risk Uncertainty & Profit*. New York: Harper & Row.

Kornai, János. 1986. The Hungarian Reform Process: Visions, Hopes, and Reality. *Journal of Economic Literature*. XXIV, 4 (Dec. 1986) : 1687–737.

Kushnirsky, F.I. 1987. Soviet Economic Reform: An Analysis and a Model. *Comparative Economic Studies*. XXIX (4): 54–85.

Lutz, Mark A., and Lux, Kenneth 1988. *Humanistic Economics: The New Challenge*. New York: Bootstrap Press.

Marx, Karl 1906. *Capital*. Volume I. Trans. S. Moore and E. Aveling. New York: Modern Library.

Marx, Karl 1967. *Capital*, Volume III, New York: International Publishers.

Marx, Karl 1972 [orig. 1847]. Wage Labour and Capital. In *The Marx–Engels Reader*. Robert C. Tucker (ed.). New York: Norton, 176–90.

Marx, Karl 1977. *Capital*. Volume I. Trans. B. Fowkes. New York: Vintage Books.

McCain, R. 1977. On the Optimum Financial Environment for Worker Cooperatives. *Zeitschrift für Nationalökonomie*. 37(3–4): 355–84.

218

McDonald, Oonagh 1989. *Own Your Own: Social Ownership Examined.* London: Unwin Paperbacks.

Menger, Anton 1899. *The Right to the Whole Produce of Labour: The Origin and Development of the Theory of Labour's Claim to the Whole Product of Industry.* Trans. M.E. Tanner. Intro. by Herbert S. Foxwell. London: Macmillan (Reprinted by Augustus Kelley).

Myrdal, Gunnar 1969. *The Political Element in the Development of Economic Theory.* Trans. by Paul Streeten. New York: Simon & Schuster.

Nove, Alec 1983. *The Economics of Feasible Socialism.* London: George Allen & Unwin.

Nozick, R. 1974. *Anarchy, State, and Utopia.* New York: Basic Books.

Nuti, Domenico Mario 1977. The Transformation of Labour Values into Production Prices and the Marxian Theory of Exploitation. In Schwartz, Jesse (ed.) 1977. *The Subtle Anatomy of Capitalism.* Santa Monica: Goodyear, 88–105.

Nuti, Domenico Mario 1988a. Perestroika. *Economic Policy: A European Forum.* 7 (October 1988) : 355–89.

Nuti, Domenico Mario 1988b. *The New Soviet Cooperatives: Advances and Limitations.* EUI Working Paper 88/362. Florence.

Oakeshott, Robert 1978. *The Case for Workers' Co-ops.* London: Routledge & Kegan Paul.

Philmore, J. 1982. The Libertarian Case for Slavery: A Note on Nozick. *Philosophical Forum.* XIV (Fall 1982) : 43–58.

Pitegoff, Peter 1987. *The Democratic ESOP.* Somerville MA: Industrial Cooperative Association.

Prasnikar, Janez, and Prasnikar, Vesna 1986. The Yugoslav Self-managed Firm in Historical Perspective. *Economic and Industrial Democracy.* 7 (1986) : 167–90.

Quarrey, M., Blasi, J. and Rosen, C. 1986. *Taking Stock: Employee Ownership at Work.* Cambridge: Ballinger.

Quirk, J., and Saposnik, R. 1968. *Introduction to General Equilibrium Theory and Welfare Economics.* New York: McGraw-Hill.

Ryan, Alan 1984. *Property and Political Theory.* Oxford: Basil Blackwell.

Sacks, Stephen 1983. *Self-management and Efficiency: Large Corporations in Yugoslavia.* London: George Allen & Unwin.

Samuelson, Paul A. 1976. *Economics.* Tenth edition. New York: McGraw-Hill.

Samuelson, Paul A. 1977. Thoughts on Profit-sharing. *Zeitschrift für die gesamte Staatswissenschaft.* (Special issue on Profit-Sharing) Vol. 133, 9–18.

Schlatter, R. 1951. *Private Property: The History of an Idea*. New Brunswick: Rutgers University Press.

Schroeder, Gertrude E. 1988. Property Rights Issues in Economic Reforms in Socialist Countries. *Studies in Comparative Communism*. XXI (Summer 1988) : 175–88.

Searle, John R. 1983. *Intentionality*. Cambridge: Cambridge University Press.

Sen, Amartya 1978. On the Labour Theory of Value: Some Methodological Issues. *Cambridge Journal of Economics*. Vol. 2 (1978), 175–90.

Shaikh, Anwar 1977. Marx's Theory of Value and the "Transformation Problem." In Schwartz, Jesse (ed.) 1977. *The Subtle Anatomy of Capitalism*. Santa Monica: Goodyear, 106–39.

Sik, Ota 1985. *For a Humane Economic Democracy*. New York: Praeger.

Speiser, Stuart M. 1985. Broadened capital ownership—the solution to major domestic and international problems. *Journal of Post Keynesian Economics*. Vol. 7, No. 3 (Spring 1985), 426–34.

Tardos, Márton 1988. How to Create Markets in Eastern Europe: The Hungarian Case. In *Economic Adjustment and Reform in Eastern Europe and the Soviet Union: Essays in Honor of Franklyn D. Holzman*. Edited by J. C. Brada, E. A. Hewett, and T. A. Wolf. 259–84. Durham: Duke University Press.

Taylor, Ian 1988. *Fair Shares for All the Workers*. London: Adam Smith Institute.

Thomas, H. and Logan, C. 1982. *Mondragon: An Economic Analysis*. London: George Allen & Unwin.

Thompson, William 1963. *An Inquiry into the Principles of the Distribution of Wealth*. (orig. published 1824). New York: Augustus Kelly.

Tomer, John F. 1987. *Organizational Capital*. New York: Praeger.

Vahcic, Ales and Petrin, Tea 1989. Financial System for Restructuring the Yugoslavian Economy. In Kessides, King, Nuti, and Sokil (eds.). *Financial Reforms in Socialist Economies.*. Washington: World Bank, 154-61.

Vanek, Jaroslav 1970. *The General Theory of Labor-Managed Market Economies*. Ithaca: Cornell University Press.

Vanek, Jaroslav 1977. *The Labor-Managed Economy*. Ithaca: Cornell University Press.

Veblen, Thorstein 1952. Veblen on Marx. In Henry W. Spiegel (ed.). *The Development of Economic Thought*. New York: Wiley, 314–28.

Walker, Martin. 1988. *The Waking Giant: Gorbachev's Russia*. New York: Pantheon Books.

References

Ward, Benjamin 1967. *The Socialist Economy*. New York: Random House.

Whyte, William Foote and Whyte, Kathleen King 1988. *Making Mondragon*. Ithaca: ILR Press.

Wiener, Hans, and Oakeshott, Robert 1987. *Worker-Owners: Mondragón Revisited*. London: Anglo-German Foundation.

Wieser, Friedrich von 1930 (Orig. 1889). *Natural Value*. Trans. Malloch, C.A. New York: G.E. Stechert & Company.

Wolff, Robert Paul 1984. *Understanding Marx*. Princeton: Princeton University Press.

Zaslavskaya, Tatyana 1989. Friends or Foes? Social forces working for and against perestroika. In *Perestroika 1989*. Edited by A. Aganbegyan. 255–78. New York: Charles Scriber's Sons.

Index

Index